ABLAZE
woe unto witchcraft
Dr. D. K. Olukoya

Setting The Covens Ablaze

WOE UNTO WITCHCRAFT

DR. D. K. OLUKOYA

SETTING THE COVENS ABLAZE

ISBN: 978-978-8424-23-9
September 2010

Published by:
Prayer city partners & Friends
MFM International Headquarters
13, Olasimbo St, UNILAG 2nd Gate,
Onike, Yaba, Lagos, Nigeria.

For Enquiries call:
Phone nos. 0805 514 5040,
0803 503 2007
0802 326 1588

All Scripture quotation is from the King James Version of the Bible

TABLE OF CONTENTS

INTRODUCTION

Prayer is a gift to you and a privilege. The gift is offered to all, and all may become the wielders of the great power in prayer. However, the fact remains that the power of prayer is least exercised by the average believer. You will do well to learn the art of warfare prayer. The present temperature of the prayer of many Christians needs to rise if they expect serious breakthroughs. The prayer points in this book are targeted at certain needs so that as you are praying you will not be beating the air. This is how to use this book:

1. Locate your area of need by looking at the table of contents.
2. Select the appropriate scriptures promising you what you desire. Meditate on them and let them sink into your spirit.
3. Go about the prayers in any of the following ways as led by the Holy Spirit:
   a. Three days' night vigil, i.e praying from 10 P.M. to 5 A.M. for three consecutive nights.
   b. Three days' fast (breaking daily), i.e. praying at intervals and breaking the fast at 6.00 P.M. or 9.00.P.M. daily.
   c. Seven days' night vigil, i.e. praying from 10 P.M. to 5 A.M. for seven consecutive nights.

d. Seven days' fast (breaking daily), i.e. praying at intervals and breaking the fast at 6.00 P.M. or 9.00.P.M. daily.

e. Three or more days of dry fast .i.e praying and fasting three or more days without any food or drink.

4. Pray aggressively.

NOTE: Spend part of the vigil or fasting, praying in the Spirit. Praying in the Spirit is the ability to pray in tongues as given utterance by the Holy Spirit. To pray in the Spirit, you must have been baptised in the Holy Ghost (not water baptism) - 1 Cor. 14:15.

You will be victorious in Jesus' name.

DEDICATION

This book is dedicated to those who have decided to join me to build for the Lord. May He build your destiny.

STRATEGIC PRAYERS FOR ATTACKING WITCHCRAFT POWERS

Areas to attack:

- Destroying their traveling routes
- Plucking off their evil eyes
- Breaking off their evil wings
- Making them to vomit the blood in their possession
- Making them to vomit the flesh in their possession
- Reversing witchcraft burial
- Destroying their mantle
- Setting their covens on fire
- Power against marine witchcraft
- Destroying their instruments
- Breaking witchcraft curses
- Vomiting their evil foods

- Power against witchcraft infirmity
- Power against witchcraft embargo on finances
- Destroying envious witchcraft
- Destroying the seat of witchcraft
- Pulling down their thrones
- Possessing the gates of the enemy

WARFARE NUMBER 1

PRAYERS AGAINST WITCHCRAFT - SPONSORED DISEASES

Witchcraft-sponsored diseases are wickedness beyond comparison. You cannot really enjoy your life on earth until you deal thoroughly with this problem.

You cannot live as ordained by God except you paralyse all the wicked witchcraft forces.

Witchcraft has no authority over you unless you give it the authority.

You should not be ignorant of the limitation of their powers, their powers are limited. Jesus has redeemed us from their powers. When Jesus said, it was finished, on the cross, the legal authority of witchcraft was neutralized. We are to enforce their defeat. Do not provide any area of your life for satanic establishment.

Submit your life unto God and exercise your authority in Jesus' name, and as a result, witchcraft will bow before you.

Note: You must be a genuine born again child of God before these prayer points can work for you. You also have to make your way plain before God by confessing your sins and asking the Lord to forgive you and wash you with the blood of Jesus.

Confessions

In the name of Jesus, I believe the word of God is steadfast and unshakeable, endures forever and is powerful. It is the power of God that is able to deliver me out of any bondage.

The word of God is God Himself speaking and not man. Therefore, nothing shall be impossible for me because of the word of God, I believe in my heart and confess with my mouth.

Father Lord, as I make this confession now, I pray that You will watch over Your word and perform it, because You are a faithful God. You are not a man that You should lie, neither the son of man that You should repent. You will not break Your covenant, nor alter the word which has gone out of Your mouth.

It is written, when I ask, I should believe and receive. As I make this confession and go into prayer, I will receive dominion and power, according to the word of God, because I know God will prove Himself strong on my behalf, for my heart is stayed on Him.

I know who I am in Christ. I have been purchased by the blood of Jesus Christ that was shed for me on the cross of calvary. I am a child of God. I am called by the name of the Lord. I am bought by the blood of the Lamb of God. I believe the power in the blood of Jesus. Jesus has translated my life from the kingdom of darkness into His marvellous kingdom of light and peace. I now belong to the kingdom of God. I have the keys of the kingdom of God in my hand to bind and to loose. I have the authority to trample under my feet, serpents, scorpions and all the powers of the enemy.

Through death, Jesus Christ has destroyed satan who had the power of death. Jesus has delivered my life from death and damnation. Before Jesus ascended, He first of all descended into the lower parts of the earth and stripped the devil of all his powers over me. Jesus has taken from satan the keys of death and hell and has given me the keys to bind and to loose.

By virtue of the work Jesus Christ did on the cross, I have power over all the powers of the enemy. He has wiped out all the handwriting of requirements that were against me, taking them out of the way, having nailed them to the cross. He disarmed principalities and power and made a show of them openly, triumphing over them in it.

I hold in my hand now the victory won for me on the cross of calvary by my Saviour Jesus Christ, and I say, be shattered, you witches and powers of wickedness and be broken in pieces. Give ears all you powers of wickedness in my place of birth or origin, gird yourselves and you shall be broken into pieces. Take your counsel together, it will come to nothing. Chant your incantations, they will not stand, for the Lord is with me as a mighty and terrible one. Therefore, you shall stumble and fall.

Encamp against me, my heart shall not fear, for in the name of the Lord, I will destroy you. The Lord is the strength of my life, of whom shall I be afraid. Surround me like bees and I will quench you all like a fire of thorns.

Fashion your weapons of wickedness, they will not prosper. Rise up against me in judgement with all your legal grounds against me, you shall all be condemned because that is my heritage as a servant of God.

I shall not die but live. Any power that has ever led me captive shall go into captivity. They that afflict and oppress me shall be ashamed. God will contend with all who contend with me. He will feed those who oppress me with their own flesh and they shall be drunk with their own blood as with sweet wine, for the Lord will bring upon them the day of doom and destroy them with double destructions.

It is written that God will light my lamp and enlighten my darkness. But every satanic agent or power oppressing me shall grope in the day-time as in thick darkness.

It is written that I should be strong in the Lord and in the power of His might, therefore, I ask that as I go into prayer right now, the Lord will be my strength, the strength to run through a troop, to leap over any wall, to pursue and overtake my enemies, to recover my stolen property, to beat them as small as the dust, to withstand and overcome all spiritual oppositions and distractions.

I hold in my hand the shield of faith, for it is written that whosoever is born of God overcometh the world. And this is the victory that overcometh the world and its wickedness, even my faith.

In faith, I go into this prayer session. In faith, I have the victory. In faith, my enemies are all subdued under my feet and none can escape.

My heart steadfastly believes the word of God. I have confessed with my mouth and by the word of my mouth, let me be justified Oh Lord, and let all my enemies be condemned. I seal my confession with the blood of Jesus. Amen.

Praise Worship

1. Let the thunder of God locate and dismantle the throne of witchcraft-sponsored diseases, in the name of Jesus.
2. Let every seat of witchcraft-sponsored diseases be roasted with the fire of God, in the name of Jesus.
3. Let the altar of witchcraft-sponsored diseases be roasted, in the name of Jesus.
4. Let the thunder of God scatter, beyond redemption, the foundation of witchcraft-sponsored diseases, in the name of Jesus.
5. Every strong-hold of witchcraft-sponsored diseases, be destroyed, in the name of Jesus.
6. Every hiding and secret places of witchcraft in my family, be

exposed by fire, in the name of Jesus.

7. Let every local and international witchcraft-sponsored diseases be shattered into pieces, in Jesus' name.
8. Let the communication system of witchcraft-sponsored diseases be shattered into pieces, in Jesus' name.
9. Let the terrible fire of God consume the transportation of witchcraft-sponsored diseases, in the name of Jesus.
10. Every agent ministering against me at the altar of witchcraft, fall down and die, in the name of Jesus.
11. Let the thunder and the fire of God locate the storehouses and strongrooms of witchcraft harboring my blessings and pull them down, in the name of Jesus.
12. Let any witchcraft curse working against me be revoked by the blood of Jesus.
13. Every decision, vow and covenant of witchcraft used against me, be revoked by the blood of Jesus, in the name of Jesus.
14. I destroy with the fire of God, every weapon of witchcraft used against me, in the name of Jesus.
15. Any material taken from my body and placed on any witchcraft altar, be roasted by the fire of God, in Jesus' name.
16. I reverse every witchcraft burial fashioned against me, in Jesus' name.

17. Every trap set for me by witches begin to catch your owners, in the name of Jesus.

18. Every witchcraft padlock fashioned against any area of my life, be roasted, in the name of Jesus.

19. Let the wisdom of witchcraft be converted to foolishness, in the name of Jesus.

20. Let the wickedness of witchcraft overturn them, in the name of Jesus.

21. I deliver my soul from every witchcraft bewitchment, in Jesus' name.

22. Any witchcraft bird flying for my sake, fall down and die and be roasted to ashes, in the name of Jesus.

23. Any of my blessing traded out by witchcraft be returned to me, in the name of Jesus.

24. Any of my blessing and testimonies swallowed by witches, be converted to hot coals of fire of God and be vomited, in Jesus' name

25. I break myself loose from every bondage of witchcraft covenants, in the name of Jesus.

26. Any witchcraft coven in which any of my blessings are hidden, be roasted by the fire of God, in the name of Jesus.

27. (Lay your right hand on your head) Every witchcraft

plantation, pollution, deposit and material in my body, be melted by the fire of God and be flushed out by the blood of Jesus.

28. Every evil ever done to me through witchcraft attack, be reversed, in the name of Jesus.

29. Every damage done to my destiny through witchcraft operations, be reversed now, in the name of Jesus.

30. Every witchcraft hand, planting evil seeds in my life through the dream, wither and burn to ashes, in the name of Jesus.

31. Every witchcraft obstacle and hindrance put on the road to my desired miracle and success, be removed by the East wind of God, in the name of Jesus.

32. Every witchcraft chant, spell and projection made against me, I bind you and turn you against your owner, in Jesus' name.

33. I frustrate every plot, device, scheme and project of witchcraft designed to affect any area of my life, in the name of Jesus.

34. Any witch projecting into the blood of any animal in order to do me harm, be trapped in the body of such an animal forever, in the name of Jesus.

35. Any drop of my blood sucked by any witch, be vomited, in the name of Jesus.

36. Any part of me shared out amongst household / village witches, I recover you, in the name of Jesus.

37. Any organ of my body that has been exchanged for another through witchcraft operations, be replaced now, in the name of Jesus.

38. I recover any of my virtues / blessings shared out amongst village / household witches, in the name of Jesus.

39. I reverse the evil effect of any witchcraft invocation or summoning of my spirit, in the name of Jesus.

40. I loose my hands and feet from any witchcraft bewitchment and bondage, in the name of Jesus.

41. Let the blood of Jesus wash away every witchcraft identification mark on me or on any of my properties, in the name of Jesus.

42. I forbid any re-union or re-gathering of household and village witches against my life, in the name of Jesus.

43. Let the entire body system of witchcraft be upset until they confess all their wickedness, in the name of Jesus.

44. Let the mercy of God be withdrawn from them, in Jesus' name.

45. Let them begin to grope in the day time as in the thick darkness, in the name of Jesus.

46.Let everything that has ever worked for them begin to work against them, in the name of Jesus.

47.Let them not have a cloth to cover their shame, in the name of Jesus.

48.Let as many of them as are stubbornly unrepentant be smitten by the sun in the day and by the moon at night, in the name of Jesus.

49.Let each step they take lead them to greater destruction, in the name of Jesus.

50.But as for me, let me dwell in the hollow of God's hand, in the name of Jesus.

51. Let the goodness and mercy of God now overwhelm me, in the name of Jesus.

52.The ministry of witchcraft in my life, family, business, career and health must die, in the name of Jesus.

53.Thunderbolt of God, begin to scatter the traveling route of any witch troubling me, in the name of Jesus.

54.Let any witchcraft route constructed against me become dark and slippery, in the name of Jesus.

55.Let life-choking thorns begin to grow on the traveling route of witchcraft-sponsored diseases, in the name of Jesus.

56.Let the traveling routes of witchcraft-sponsored diseases become their burial places, in the name of Jesus.

57. Let the angels of destruction continually minister on any route of witchcraft that is fashioned against me, in the name of Jesus.

58. Every witchcraft eye monitoring my business for destruction, be plucked out by fire, in the name of Jesus.

59. Every witchcraft eye manipulating my finances, be plucked off, in the name of Jesus.

60. Every witchcraft eye manipulating my spiritual life, be cut off, in the name of Jesus.

61. Let the eyes of every household witchcraft manipulating my marriage be plucked off by fire, in the name of Jesus.

62. Arrows of fire, pluck out the eyes of every monitoring agent over the affairs of my life, in the name of Jesus.

63. Witchcraft spirit from the North, the South, the West, and the East, holding on to my flesh, release it now, in the name of Jesus.

64. As fish vomited Jonah to the dry land, any witchcraft that has swallowed me, vomit me now, in the name of Jesus.

65. Any area of my life, swallowed by rebellious spirits, be vomited by fire, in the name of Jesus.

66. Any witchcraft that has swallowed my health, vomit it now, in

the name of Jesus.

67. I jump out of my parents, my parents, jump out of my life, in the name of Jesus.

68. Every operation of witchcraft burial in my life, be reversed now, in the name of Jesus.

69. Every witchcraft burial against my health, be reversed now, in the name of Jesus.

70. Oh Lord, let the power of witchcraft burial against my health be reversed now, in the name of Jesus.

71. My health that has been buried in the dark world, be reversed now, in Jesus' name.

72. My God, deliver me from every witchcraft fashioned against my health, in the name of Jesus.

73. Every mantle of witchcraft in my family, be roasted, in Jesus' name.

74. I reject every witchcraft influence, in the name of Jesus.

75. I reject every witchcraft inheritance, in the name of Jesus.

76. Every witchcraft kingdom in my household, I destroy you by fire, in the name of Jesus.

77. I refuse to operate under witchcraft dominion, in Jesus' name.

78. Oh Lord, let Your thunder and fire locate all the covens of

witches and wizards established against me for total destruction.

79. As the wax is melted by fire, let all witchcraft covens caging my life or destiny evaporate by fire, in the name of Jesus.

80. All witchcraft banks and strongroom harboring my health, be pulled down by fire, in the name of Jesus.

81. Oh Lord, my God, let Your fire fall and consume every witchcraft assembly frustrating God's plan for my life, in the name of Jesus.

82. Every stronghold of witches and wizards in my place of birth (mention the name of the place), I dismantle you by fire, in the name of Jesus.

83. Every marine witchcraft present in my family, be disgraced by fire, in the name of Jesus.

84. I break the backbone of every marine witchcraft militating against my life with the hands of life, in the name of Jesus.

85. Every work of marine witchcraft in my life, be destroyed by the blood of Jesus.

86. I release my life from the grip of marine witchcraft, in Jesus' name.

87. Every mark of witchcraft in my life, be wiped off by the blood of Jesus.

88.Let the rod and staff of witchcraft spirit operating against my life, break into pieces, in the name of Jesus.

89.I command every evil pot and concoction used against my life to break into pieces, in the name of Jesus.

90.Let every dark forest, hiding witchcraft weapons against me, burn to ashes, in the name of Jesus.

91. Evil mirrors, used to monitor my life, crush into pieces, in Jesus' name.

92.Let the horn, tooth and needle of witchcraft spirit used against my life, be destroyed irreparably, in the name of Jesus.

93.(Raise your two hands up) Father Lord, baptize my hand with your liquid fire mixed with the blood of Jesus to destroy and break witchcraft curses, in the name of Jesus.

94.(Lay the two hands on your head now) Father Lord, destroy every witchcraft curse upon my life by your fire, in the name of Jesus.

95.You my divine destiny, you will not be bewitched, in Jesus' name.

96.I gather together every witchcraft curse issued against my life and I send them back to the sender, in the name of Jesus.

97.You spirit and demons backing up witchcraft in my life, somersault, fall down and die, in the name of Jesus.

98.Father Lord, let my intestine and every organ of my body experience the fireworks of the Holy Ghost, in Jesus' name.

99.Father Lord, in the name of Jesus, I vomit every evil food that I have eaten.

100. Let the blood of Jesus flush out every poison deposited in my blood system as a result of evil food, in Jesus' name.

101. All that I have lost as a result of eating evil food, Father Lord, let me have them back, in the name of Jesus.

102. Oh God, re-arrange any part of my body that has been fragmented by the power of infirmity, in the name of Jesus.

103. I curse to die, you the power of infirmity working in any part of my body, in the name of Jesus.

104. I speak destruction to the root of any infirmity planted by witchcraft powers into my life, in the name of Jesus.

105. Every inherited sickness from my family lineage, dry to your root, in the name of Jesus.

106. Lay your right hand on any part where you have infirmity and say the following: Vanish from my body (three times), in the name of Jesus), hypertension, evil growth, plantation

of evil growth, cancer, unidentified sickness.

107. Anything in me, supporting witchcraft embargoes on my health, come out with all your roots, in Jesus' name.

108. Owners of evil loads of witchcraft embargoes, carry your load, in the name of Jesus.

109. Every ancestral embargo on my health, I break you, in the name of Jesus.

110. I recover my finances from witchcraft embargoes, in Jesus' name.

111. Let every envious witchcraft activity set in motion against my advancement, be destroyed by fire, in Jesus' name.

112. Let every envious witchcraft agent from my place of birth, fall down and die, in the name of Jesus.

113. Let all envious witchcraft agents militating against my progress, be sentenced to their grave, in Jesus' name.

114. I blind the eyes of envious witchcraft agents monitoring my life, in the name of Jesus.

115. You envious witchcraft power, release my life now, in Jesus' name.

116. Everyone that planted evil seeds of witchcraft upon my life, I command you to receive the spirit of confusion now, in the name of Jesus.

117. Thunder fire of God, destroy every seat of witchcraft stronghold that I inherited, in the name of Jesus.

118. I break down and burn to ashes, every seat of witchcraft stronghold that I have built with my own mouth and I cancel their effects upon my life, in the name of Jesus.

119. Father Lord, let every inherited seat of witchcraft presently working against my life be roasted by fire, in Jesus' name.

120. Every blessing of my family, my life, my marriage, my business, spiritual and physical life that witchcraft stronghold has eaten up, be released now, in the name of Jesus.

121. Every throne of witchcraft in my neighbourhood, be pulled down, in the name of Jesus.

122. Every flying throne of witchcraft, be cast down, in Jesus' name.

123. Every throne of witchcraft, set up against my enthronement, be demolished, in the name of Jesus.

124. Let the throne of Jesus Christ be established in every area of my life, in the name of Jesus.

125. Today and now, I possess the gates of my enemies, in Jesus' name.

126. Oh Lord, use Your broom of destruction to sweep away the habitation of witchcraft in my life.

127. I capture by fire, the key of my beneficial potential from the custody of witchcraft-sponsored diseases, in the name of Jesus.

128. Oh Lord, make me a terror and a problem to witchcraft-sponsored diseases, in the name of Jesus.

129. I retrieve my blessing from the hand of evil confiscators, in the name of Jesus.

130. Every drop of my blood in witchcraft coven, catch fire, in the name of Jesus.

131. I dislodge and set on fire, every witchcraft army assigned against my life, in the name of Jesus.

132. Every witchcraft parasite in my blood, die, in Jesus' name.

133. Every evil current of witchcraft in my blood, be drained out now, in the name of Jesus.

134. Begin to bless the name of the Lord for answering your prayer.

WARFARE NUMBER 2

KILLING THE WITCHCRAFT IN YOUR DESTINY

CONFESSION: Matthew 15:13: But he answered and said, Every plant, which my heavenly Father hath not planted, shall be rooted up.

1. Let as many of them as are stubbornly unrepentant be smitten by the sun in the day and by the moon in the night, in the name of Jesus.
2. Let each step they take lead them to greater destruction, in the name of Jesus.
3. But as for me, let me dwell in the hollow of God's hand, in the name of Jesus.
4. Let the goodness and mercy of God now overwhelm me, in the name of Jesus.
5. Any witchcraft practised under any water against my life, receive immediate judgment of fire, in the name of Jesus.
6. Every witchcraft power that has introduced spirit husband/wife or child into my dreams be roasted by fire, in Jesus' name.
7. Every agent of witchcraft power posing as my husband, wife or child in my dreams, be roasted by fire, in Jesus' name.
8. Every agent of witchcraft power physically attached to my marriage to frustrate it, fall down and perish now, in the name of Jesus.

9. Every agent of witchcraft power assigned to attack my finances through the dream, fall down and perish, in the name of Jesus.

10. Let the thunderbolts of God locate and destroy every witchcraft power covens where deliberations and decisions are fashioned against me, in the name of Jesus.

11. Any water spirit from my village, in my place of birth, practising witchcraft against me and my family, be amputated by the Word of God, in the name of Jesus.

12. Any power of witchcraft holding any of my blessings in bondage, receive the fire of God and release them, in the name of Jesus.

13. I loose my mind and soul from the bondage of marine witches, in the name of Jesus.

14. Any witchcraft power chain, binding my hands and feet from prospering, be broken and shattered into pieces, in the name of Jesus.

15. Every arrow shot into my life from under any water through witchcraft, come out of me and go back to your sender, in the name of Jesus.

16. Any evil material transferred into my body, through contact with any witchcraft agent, be roasted by fire, in the name of Jesus.

17. Any evil done against me so far through witchcraft power of oppression and manipulation, be reversed by the blood of Jesus.

18. I bind every witchcraft control and mind-blinding spirit, in the name of Jesus.

19. I cast out every witchcraft arrow affecting my senses (sight, smell, taste, hearing), in the name of Jesus.

20. I command every witchcraft arrow to depart from my ___, in the name of Jesus.

- spinal cord - spleen - navel - heart - throat
- eyes - top of the head.

21. Let the blood of Jesus purge me of every witchcraft contaminating material, in the name of Jesus.

22. I destroy the hand of any witch-doctor working against me, in the name of Jesus.

23. Every witchcraft spirit attempting to build a wall against my destiny, fall down and die, in the name of Jesus.

24. I send the rain of affliction upon every witchcraft power working against me, in the name of Jesus.

25. O sun, moon, stars, earth, water and the elements, vomit every enchantment that is against me, in the name of Jesus

26. Every power using the heavenlies against me, fall down and be

disgraced, in the name of Jesus.

27. Let the stars of heaven begin to fight for me, in the name of Jesus.

28. Oh God, arise and scatter every conspiracy in the heavenlies that is against me, in the name of Jesus.

29. I break with the blood of Jesus all evil soul-ties affecting my life, in the name of Jesus.

30. Spirit of the Living God, come upon my life and place a shield of protection around me, in the name of Jesus.

31. Every chain of inherited witchcraft in my family, break, in the name of Jesus.

32. Every ladder used by witchcraft against me, be roasted, in the name of Jesus.

33. Any door that I have opened to witchcraft in any area of my life, be closed for ever by the blood of Jesus.

34. I revoke every witchcraft verdict on my marital life, in the name of Jesus.

35. I send confusion into the camp of household witchcraft, in the name of Jesus.

36. Stubborn witchcraft, release me, in the name of Jesus.

37. Every witchcraft power, working against my destiny, fall down and die, in the name of Jesus.

38.Every incantation, ritual and witchcraft power against my destiny, fall down and die, in Jesus' name.

39.I break the power of the occult, witchcraft and familiar spirits over my life, in the name of Jesus.

40.Witchcraft opposition, receive the rain of affliction, in the name of Jesus.

41. I cancel every witchcraft verdict against my life, in the name of Jesus.

42.I command every arrow of witchcraft in my life, come out with all your roots in the name of Jesus! (Lay your hands on your stomach and pray aggressively.)

43.I command every witchcraft pot, using remote control against my health to be broken into pieces, in the name of Jesus.

44.I rebuke, the spell of any witchcraft pot from my neck, in the name of Jesus.

45.I break every witchcraft pot over my life, in the name of Jesus.

46.Every council of witchcraft working against me will not prosper, in the name of Jesus.

47. I release myself and my family from every witchcraft cage and pot, in the name of Jesus.

48.I retrieve my integrity out of the hands of household

witchcraft, in the name of Jesus.

49. Every witchcraft hand, planting evil seeds in my life through attacks in the dream, wither and burn to ashes, in the name of Jesus.

50. Let all friendly witchcraft powers be exposed and be disgraced, in the name of Jesus.

51. Oh Lord, plant Your warring angels around me to dismantle and destroy evil stronghold of internal witchcraft.

52. I exercise my authority over stubborn witchcraft and I pull down their structures, in the name of Jesus.

53. Every witchcraft targeting my placenta against my destiny, what are you waiting for? die, in the name of Jesus.

54. Every witchcraft using my placenta to manipulate my destiny, die, in the name of Jesus.

55. Every blessing that I have lost through placental witchcraft, I possess you, in Jesus' name.

56. Every witchcraft coven and marine banks, release my placenta, in Jesus' name

57. Every cage of family witchcraft, release my divine partner, in Jesus' name.

58. Oh Lord, let my dreams and visions reject every witchcraft projection, in the name of Jesus.

WARFARE NUMBER 3

DEALING WITH ANTI-PROMOTION WITCHCRAFT

CONFESSION: Psalm 119:15

Praise Worship

1. I revoke every satanic decree, issued against my promotion, in the name of Jesus.
2. I silence, every evil dog barking against my breakthroughs, in the name of Jesus.
3. Let the finger of God, unseat my household strongman, in the name of Jesus.
4. Let every evil bird, flying for my sake, be trapped, in the name of Jesus.
5. Every agent of disgrace, backwardness and shame, release me, in the name of Jesus.
6. I overthrow every evil throne installed against my life, in the name of Jesus.
7. Every agent of disorder in my life, be scattered unto desolation, in the name of Jesus.
8. Every power fuelling my problems, fall down and die, in the name of Jesus.
9. I release myself from any curse, working in my family, in the name of Jesus.
10. Let every spiritual vulture delegated against me, eat their own flesh, in the name of Jesus.

11. I receive the shoes of iron and trample upon serpents and scorpions, in the name of Jesus.
12. Every cleverly concealed root of problem, be uprooted, in the name of Jesus.
13. I disgrace every evil wisdom working against my breakthroughs, in the name of Jesus.
14. In the power of the Holy Spirit, I crush all my enemies, in the name of Jesus.
15. In the power of the Holy Spirit, I put every evil under my feet, in the name of Jesus.
16. Lord, let me be extraordinary, in the name of Jesus.
17. Holy Spirit, deposit Your wonders in my life, in the name of Jesus.
18. Lord Jesus, break my infirmity and destroy my disease.
19. Lord Jesus, destroy satanic foundations and build me upon Your word.
20. Lord Jesus, set me ablaze with Your Spirit.
21. Let divine earthquake shake down the foundation of every satanic prison, in the name of Jesus.
22. I loose confusion, shame and reproach into the camp of the enemy, in the name of Jesus.

23.I bind every evil spirit withstanding good testimonies in my life, in the name of Jesus.

24.Let every satanic river of backwardness dry up, in the name of Jesus.

25.I destroy every evil dedication made by my parents for my sake, in the name of Jesus.

26.Let all prayer failure, cease in my life, in the name of Jesus.

27.Holy Ghost, fulfil Your purpose in me now, in the name of Jesus.

28.I refuse to be moved by environmental situations or satanic revival, in the name of Jesus.

29.I will receive all that the Lord has purposed for me in this programme, in the name of Jesus.

30.Oh Lord, create within me a hunger and thirst for purity and holiness, in the name of Jesus.

31. Holy Spirit, promote divine possibility in my life, in the name of Jesus.

32.Holy Spirit, liberate my spirit that I may scorn the works of the flesh, in the name of Jesus.

33.I put the thoughts of accusation against my captive, in the name of Jesus.

34.I command everything working contrary to the obedience of

Christ in my life to wither away, in the name of Jesus.

35.Holy Spirit, transform me from weakness to strength, in the name of Jesus.

36.Holy Spirit, unmask any portion of me that is not surrendered, in the name of Jesus.

37.Holy Spirit, begin to expose all the hidden sins in my life, in the name of Jesus.

WARFARE NUMBER 4

DEALING WITH DOMESTIC WITCHCRAFT

CONFESSIONS

Psalms 18:37: I have pursued mine enemies, and overtaken them: neither did I turn again till they were consumed.

Obadiah 1:3-4: The pride of thine heart hath deceived thee, thou that dwellest in the clefts of the rock, whose habitation is high; that saith in his heart, Who shall bring me down to the ground? Though thou exalt thyself as the eagle, and though thou set thy nest among the stars, thence will I bring thee down, saith the LORD.

Isaiah 54:17: No weapon that is formed against thee shall prosper; and every tongue that shall rise against thee in judgment thou shalt condemn. This is the heritage of the servants of the LORD, and their righteousness is of me, saith the LORD.

Luke 10:19: Behold, I give unto you power to tread on serpents and scorpions, and over all the power of the enemy, and nothing shall by any means hurt you.

Jeremiah 1:19: And they shall fight against thee; but they shall not prevail against thee; for I am with thee, saith the LORD, to deliver thee.

Praise worship

1. Thank the Lord for His power that is available to open your spiritual eyes.

2. Thank the Lord for the power in the blood of Jesus to save, to heal and to deliver.
3. Let my environment become too hot for any private enemy, in the name of Jesus.
4. Let all friendly witchcraft powers be exposed and disgraced, in the name of Jesus.
5. Every cooperation from the spirit of darkness around me, scatter, in the name of Jesus.
6. Lord, let Your light expose every hidden evil structure planted around me.
7. I shall arise and go forth, in the name of Jesus.
8. Any evil tree planted around me, be uprooted, in the name of Jesus.
9. I dismantle the powers stealing from the garden of my life, in the name of Jesus.
10. Every veil of darkness, be roasted by the fire of God, in the name of Jesus.
11. Let the source of the power of unfriendly friends be dissolved by the fire of God, in the name of Jesus.
12. I shake off any evil thing deposited into my body by friendly enemies, in the name of Jesus.
13. God, arise in Your power and confuse my close oppressors, in

the name of Jesus.

14. Lord, plant Your warring angels around me to dismantle and destroy evil stronghold of internal witchcraft.

15. Let my enemies make mistakes that would advance my course, in the name of Jesus.

16. Anything that the Father has not planted in my immediate environment, be uprooted, in Jesus' name

17. Listen to me satan, I plead the blood of Jesus over this environment.

18. Lord, take absolute control over my body, soul and spirit, in the name of Jesus.

19. Lord Jesus, I surrender every part of my life to You.

20. I receive the anointing of the warrior to drink the blood of the enemy, in the name of Jesus.

21. I charge my spiritual battle by the fire of the Holy Ghost, in the name of Jesus.

22. I challenge and destroy every satanic operation against my prayer life, in the name of Jesus.

23. I reject, every involvement of the flesh and satan in my prayer, in the name of Jesus.

24. God, arise and let every evil presence around me scatter, in the name of Jesus.

25.Every power blocking me from the will of God, fall down and die, in the name of Jesus.

26.I pull down every stubborn stronghold protecting my enemy, in the name of Jesus.

27.I arrest every spirit of confusion by fire, in the name of Jesus.

28.I bring the blood of Jesus between me and the powers of darkness, in the name of Jesus.

29.Every problem (name it) harassing my life, I break your backbone by fire, in the name of Jesus.

30.I release myself from every evil spirit behind the problem (name it), in the name of Jesus.

31. Let the backbone of the strongman in charge of each problem be broken, in the name of Jesus.

32.Every evil flame, fueling my problem, be disgraced by the blood of Jesus.

33.I command every evil monitoring spirit to leave me now, in the name of Jesus.

34.I renounce satan and his host, and declare them to be my enemies, in the name of Jesus.

35.I exercise my authority over stubborn witchcraft and I pull down their structures, in Jesus' name

36. Listen to me satan, because of the blood of Jesus, you have no more power over me, no more place in me, in the name of Jesus.

37. I place the blood of Jesus upon myself and my family, in the name of Jesus.

38. I draw the bloodline of the Lord Jesus Christ around all my possessions, in the name of Jesus.

39. I draw the bloodline of Jesus around all my possessions and property, in the name of Jesus.

40. O Rock of Ages, smash to pieces every foundation of witchcraft in my family, in the name of Jesus.

41. Let witchcraft powers eat their own flesh and drink their own blood, in the name of Jesus.

42. Every seat of witchcraft, receive the thunder fire of God, in the name of Jesus.

43. Let the habitation of witchcraft powers be desolate, in the name of Jesus.

44. Every throne of witchcraft, be dismantled by fire, in Jesus' name

45. Let the stronghold of witchcraft powers be pulled down by fire, in the name of Jesus.

46. Let the refuge of witchcraft powers be pulled down by fire,

in Jesus' name.

47.Let the network of witchcraft disintegrate, in Jesus' name.

48.Let the communication systems of witchcraft powers, be destroyed by fire, in the name of Jesus.

49.Every transportation system of witchcraft powers, be destroyed by fire, in the name of Jesus.

50.Let the weapons of witchcraft powers turn against them, in the name of Jesus.

51. I withdraw my blessings from every bank or strongroom of the enemy, in the name of Jesus.

52.Oh altar of witchcraft, break, in the name of Jesus.

53.Every witchcraft padlock fashioned against me, break by fire, in the name of Jesus.

54.Every trap of witchcraft, catch your owners, in Jesus' name.

55.Every witchcraft utterance and projection made against me, be overthrown, in the name of Jesus.

56.I reverse every witchcraft burial fashioned against me, in the name of Jesus.

57.I deliver my soul from every witchcraft bewitchment, in the name of Jesus.

58.I reverse the effect of every witchcraft summoning of my

spirit, in the name of Jesus.

59. Every witchcraft identification mark, be wiped off by the blood of Jesus.

60. I frustrate every witchcraft exchange of my virtues, in the name of Jesus.

61. Let the blood of Jesus block the flying route of witchcraft powers targeted against me.

62. Let every witchcraft curse break and be destroyed, in Jesus' name.

63. Every covenant of witchcraft, melt by the blood of Jesus.

64. I withdraw every organ of my body from any witchcraft altar, in the name of Jesus.

65. Anything planted in my life by witchcraft, come out and die, in the name of Jesus.

66. Let the blood of Jesus cancel every witchcraft initiation fashioned against my destiny, in Jesus' name

67. Every witchcraft poison, be destroyed, in the name of Jesus.

68. I reverse every witchcraft pattern fashioned against my destiny, in the name of Jesus.

69. Every witchcraft cage, fashioned against my life, be destroyed, in the name of Jesus.

70.Let every problem in my life that originated from witchcraft, receive divine and instant solution, in the name of Jesus.

71. I command all the damages done to my life by witchcraft to be repaired, in the name of Jesus.

72.Let every blessing confiscated by witchcraft spirits be released, in Jesus' name.

73.Every witchcraft power assigned against my life and marriage, receive ___ (pick from the under listed), in Jesus' name.

- the thunder and lightning of God
- unbearable heat
- raging fire
- hail and fire mingled with the blood of the Lamb
- concentrated acid
- continuous plagues
- destroying flood
- destruction
- failure
- confusion

74.I loose myself, from any power of witchcraft, in Jesus' name.

75.Every camp of witchcraft, gathered against my prosperity, fall down and die, in Jesus' name.

76.Every witchcraft pot working against me, I bring the judgment of God against you, in Jesus' name.

77.I command every witchcraft pot using remote control against my health to be broken into pieces, in Jesus' name.

78. Witchcraft opposition, receive the rain of affliction, in the name of Jesus.

79. Let the spirit of witchcraft attack the familiar spirits fashioned against me, in Jesus' name.

80. I retrieve my integrity out of the hands of household witchcraft, in the name of Jesus.

81. I break the power of the occult, witchcraft and familiar spirits over my life, in Jesus' name.

82. In the name of Jesus, I break and loose myself from all evil curses, chains, spells, jinx, bewitchments, witchcraft or sorcery which may have been put upon me.

83. Let the thunder of God locate and dismantle the throne of witchcraft in my household, in Jesus' name.

84. Let every seat of witchcraft in my household, be roasted by the fire of God, in Jesus' name.

85. Let the altar of witchcraft in my household be roasted, in Jesus' name.

86. Let the thunder of God scatter beyond redemption, the foundation of witchcraft in my household, in Jesus' name.

87. Every stronghold of refuge of my household witches, be destroyed, in the name of Jesus.

88. Every hiding and secret places of witchcraft in my family, be

exposed by fire, in the name of Jesus.

89.Let every local and international witchcraft network of my household witches, be shattered into pieces, in Jesus' name.

90.Let the communication system of my household witches be frustrated, in the name of Jesus.

91. Let the terrible fire of God, consume the transportation of my household witchcraft, in Jesus' name.

92.Every agent ministering at the altar of witchcraft in my household, fall down and die, in Jesus' name.

93.Let the thunder and the fire of God, locate the storehouses and strongrooms of the household witchcraft harbouring my blessings, and pull them down, in the name of Jesus.

94.Let any witchcraft curse, working against me, be revoked by the blood of Jesus.

95.Every decision, vow and covenant of household witchcraft affecting me, be nullified by the blood of Jesus.

96.I destroy with the fire of God, every weapon of witchcraft used against me, in Jesus' name.

97.Any material taken from my body and now placed on a witchcraft altar, be roasted by the fire of God, in Jesus' name.

98.I reverse every witchcraft burial fashioned against me, in the

name of Jesus.

99. Every trap set for me by witches, begin to catch your owners, in the name of Jesus.

100. Every witchcraft padlock, fashioned against any area of my life, be roasted, in Jesus' name.

101. Let the wisdom of household witches, be converted to foolishness, in the name of Jesus.

102. Let the wickedness of household enemies, overtake them, in the name of Jesus.

103. I deliver my soul from every witchcraft bewitchment, in the name of Jesus.

104. Any witchcraft bird flying for my sake, fall down, die and be roasted to ashes, in the name of Jesus.

105. Any of my blessings traded with, by household witches, be returned to me, in Jesus' name.

106. Any of my blessings and testimonies swallowed by witches, be converted to hot coals of fire of God and be vomited, in the name of Jesus.

107. I break myself loose from every bondage of witchcraft covenants, in the name of Jesus.

108. Any witchcraft coven where any of my blessings are hidden, be roasted by the fire of God, in the name of

Jesus.

109. (Lay your right hand on your head) Every witchcraft spirit plantation, pollution, deposit and material in my body, melt by the fire of God and be flushed out by the blood of Jesus.

110. Every witchcraft hand planting evil seeds in my life through attacks in the dream, wither and burn to ashes, in Jesus' name.

111. Every witchcraft obstacle put on the road to my desired miracle and success, be removed by the east wind of God, in Jesus' name.

112. Every witchcraft chant, spell and projection made against me, I bind you and turn you against your owner, in the name of Jesus.

113. I frustrate every plot, device, scheme and project of witchcraft designed to affect any area of my life, in the name of Jesus.

114. Any witch projecting himself into the body of any animal in order to do me harm, be trapped in the body of such an animal forever, in the name of Jesus.

115. Any drop of my blood sucked by any witch, be vomited now, in the name of Jesus.

116. Any part of me shared out amongst household/ village witches, I recover you, in the name of Jesus.

117. Any organ of my body that has been exchanged for another through witchcraft operation, be replaced now, in the name of Jesus.

118. I recover any of my virtues/ blessings shared out amongst village/ household witches, in Jesus' name.

119. I reverse the evil effect of any witchcraft invocation or summoning of my spirit, in the name of Jesus.

120. I loose my hands and feet from any witchcraft bewitchment or bondage, in Jesus' name.

121. Let the blood of Jesus wash away every witchcraft identification mark on me or on any of my properties, in the name of Jesus.

122. I forbid any re-union or re-gathering of household and village witches against my life, in Jesus' name.

123. Let the entire body system of my household witches begin to run amok until they confess all their wickedness, in Jesus' name.

124. Let the mercy of God be withdrawn from them, in Jesus' name.

125. Let them begin to grope in the daytime as in the thickness

of a dark night, in the name of Jesus.

126. Let everything that has ever worked for them begin to work against them, in Jesus' name.

127. Let them not have a cloth to cover their shame, in Jesus' name

128. Let as many of them that are stubbornly unrepentant, be smitten by the sun in the day and by the moon, in the night in Jesus' name.

129. Let each step they take lead them to greater destruction, in the name of Jesus.

130. But as for me, let me dwell in the hollow of God's hand, in the name of Jesus.

131. Let the goodness and mercy of God overwhelm me now, in the name of Jesus.

132. Any witchcraft operation under any water against my life, receive immediate judgment of fire, in the name of Jesus.

133. Every witchcraft power that has introduced spirit husband/ wife or child into my dreams, be roasted by fire, in the name of Jesus.

134. Every agent of witchcraft power, posing as my husband/ wife or child in my dreams, be roasted by fire, in Jesus' name.

135. Every agent of witchcraft power, physically attached to my marriage to frustrate it, fall down now and perish, in Jesus' name.

136. Every agent of witchcraft power, assigned to attack my finances through the dream, fall down and perish, in Jesus' name.

137. Let the thunderbolts of God, locate and destroy every witchcraft power coven, where deliberations and decisions were fashioned against me, in the name of Jesus.

138. Any water spirit from my village or place of birth, practicing witchcraft against me and my family, be amputated by the word of God, in the name of Jesus.

139. Any power of witchcraft, holding any of my blessings in bondage, receive the fire of God and release them, in the name of Jesus.

140. I loose my mind and soul, from the bondage of marine witches, in the name of Jesus.

141. Any witchcraft power chain, binding my hands and feet from prospering, be shattered into pieces, in Jesus' name.

142. Every arrow, shot into my life from under any water through witchcraft, come out of me and go back to your sender, in the name of Jesus.

143. Any evil material, transferred into my body, through contact with any witchcraft agent, roast by fire, in the name of Jesus.

144. Any evil done against me through witchcraft oppression or manipulation, be reversed by the blood of Jesus.

145. I bind every witchcraft control and mind-blinding spirit, in the name of Jesus.

146. I cast out every witchcraft arrow affecting my senses (sight, smell, taste, hearing), in the name of Jesus.

147. I command every witchcraft arrow to depart from my

- Spinal cord - spleen - navel - heart - throat

- eyes - head, in the name of Jesus.

148. Let the blood of Jesus purge me of every witchcraft contaminating material, in the name of Jesus.

149. I destroy the hand of any witch-doctor working against me, in the name of Jesus.

150. Every witchcraft spirit attempting to build a wall against my destiny, fall down and die, in Jesus' name.

151. I send the rain of affliction upon every witchcraft power working against me, in the name of Jesus.

152. Oh sun, moon, stars, earth, water and the elements, vomit every enchantment that is against me, in the name of

Jesus.

153. Every power using the heavenlies against me, fall down and be disgraced, in Jesus' name.

154. Let the stars of heaven begin to fight for me, in Jesus' name.

155. Oh God, arise and scatter every conspiracy in the heavenlies that is against me, in Jesus' name.

156. I break, with the blood of Jesus, all evil soul-ties affecting my life, in the name of Jesus.

157. Spirit of the Living God, come upon my life and place a shield of protection around me, in Jesus' name.

158. Every chain of inherited witchcraft in my family, break, in the name of Jesus.

159. Every ladder used by witchcraft against me, be roasted, in the name of Jesus.

160. Any door, that I have opened to witchcraft in any area of my life, be closed for ever by the blood of Jesus.

161. I revoke, every witchcraft verdict, on my marital life, in the name of Jesus.

162. I send confusion, into the camp of household witchcraft, in the name of Jesus.

163. Stubborn witchcraft, release me, in the name of Jesus.

164. Every witchcraft power working against my destiny, fall down and die, in Jesus' name.

165. Every incantation, ritual and witchcraft power against my destiny, fall down and die, in the name of Jesus.

166. I break the power of the occult, witchcraft and familiar spirits over my life, in Jesus' name.

167. Witchcraft opposition, receive the rain of affliction, in the name of Jesus.

168. I cancel every witchcraft verdict against my life, in Jesus' name.

169. I command every arrow of witchcraft in my life; Come out with all your roots, in the name of Jesus. (Lay your hands on your stomach and pray aggressively).

170. I command every witchcraft pot, using remote control against my health to be broken into pieces, in Jesus' name.

171. I rebuke the spell of any witchcraft pot from my neck, in the name of Jesus.

172. I break every witchcraft pot over my life, in Jesus' name.

173. Every council of witchcraft, working against me, will not prosper, in Jesus' name.

174. I release myself and my family from every witchcraft cage and pot, in Jesus' name.

175. I retrieve my integrity from the hands of household witchcraft, in Jesus' name.

176. Every witchcraft hand, planting evil seeds in my life through attacks in the dream, wither and burn to ashes, in Jesus' name.

177. Let all friendly witchcraft powers be exposed and disgraced, in Jesus' name.

178. Oh Lord, plant your warring angels around me to dismantle and destroy evil stronghold of internal witchcraft.

179. I exercise my authority over stubborn witchcraft and I pull down its structure, in Jesus' name.

180. Every placenta witchcraft targeted against my destiny, what are you waiting for? die, in Jesus' name.

181. Placenta witchcraft manipulating my destiny, die, in Jesus' name.

182. Every blessing that I have lost through placenta witchcraft, I repossess you, in Jesus' name.

183. Every witchcraft coven and marine bank, release my placenta, in Jesus' name.

184. Every cage of family witchcraft, release my divine partner, in Jesus' name.

185. Oh Lord, let my dreams and visions reject every

witchcraft projection, in Jesus' name.

186. Thank God for answers to your prayers.

WARFARE NUMBER 5

DEALING WITH WITCHCRAFT WICKEDNESS

Confessions:

Isaiah 54:17: No weapon that is formed against thee shall prosper; and every tongue that shall rise against thee in judgment thou shalt condemn. This is the heritage of the servants of the Lord, and their righteousness is of me, saith the Lord.

Isaiah 54:15: Behold, they shall surely gather together, but not by me: whosoever shall gather together against thee shall fall for thy sake.

Psalm 91:13: Thou shalt tread upon the lion and adder: the young lion and the dragon shalt thou trample under feet.

Jeremiah 33:3: Call unto me, and I will answer thee, and shew thee great and mighty things, which thou knowest not.

Jeremiah 29:11: For I know the thoughts that I think toward you, saith the Lord, thoughts of peace, and not of evil, to give you an expected end.

Micah 7:8: Rejoice not against me, O mine enemy: when I fall, I shall arise; when I sit in darkness, the Lord shall be a light unto me.

Jeremiah 1:19: And they shall fight against thee; but they shall not prevail against thee; for I am with thee, saith the Lord, to deliver thee.

Psalm 91:10: There shall no evil befall thee, neither shall any plague come nigh thy dwelling.

1 Samuel 17:47: And all this assembly shall know that the Lord saveth not with sword and spear: for the battle is the Lord's, and he will give you into our hands.

Psalm 23:4: Yea, though I walk through the valley of the shadow of death, I will fear no evil: for thou art with me; thy rod and thy staff they comfort me.

Psalm 22:8: He trusted on the Lord that he would deliver him: let him deliver him, seeing he delighted in him.

Obadiah 1:17: But upon mount Zion shall be deliverance, and there shall be holiness; and the house of Jacob shall possess their possessions.

Praise Worship

1. Lord Jesus, I submit myself to You, fully, as I go into prayers, in the name of Jesus.
2. I ask that every part of me be energized and strengthened for warfare, in the name of Jesus.
3. I put all my angels to war to fight for me throughout this period and even afterwards, in the name of Jesus.
4. I renounce for myself, and on behalf of my family, any satanic witchcraft initiation we are into, either consciously or unconsciously, in the name of Jesus.

5. I break every witchcraft curse, spell, pronouncement, manipulation, intimidation, and domination, in my life and family, in the name of Jesus.
6. I loose and free myself and members of my family from all sorts of witchcraft imprisonment, in the name of Jesus.
7. It is written, suffer not a witch to live. I suffer not a witch or wizard against my life to live, in the name of Jesus.
8. I loose my health from witchcraft curses. Any sickness planted in my body, by witches, today, I cast you out, in the name of Jesus.
9. I loose my finances and businesses from witchcraft entanglement and imprisonments, in the name of Jesus.
10. I loose my husband/wife, children, from witchcraft oppression, in the name of Jesus.
11. I release the eastern thunderous wind of God on every witchcraft coven meeting that is against me and my family, in the name of Jesus.
12. I throw down all witchcraft cauldrons and concoctions boiled on my behalf, in the name of Jesus.
13. I open every padlock locked up against me by witches and wizards, in the name of Jesus.
14. It is written, let God arise and let His enemies be scattered.

I invoke the power of God against the power of witches, in the name of Jesus.

15. I release the unquenchable fire of the Holy Ghost, the earthquake of God, the thunder and brimstone of God against the camp of my enemies, in the name of Jesus.

16. I paralyze, neutralize and overrule the powers of the enemies against my life, in the name of Jesus.

17. I destroy every organized network of demonic wickedness against me, in the name of Jesus.

18. I pray down the deliverance power of God by the Holy Spirit upon my life, in the name of Jesus.

19. I loose myself and my family from ancestral witchcraft, marine witchcraft, occultic witchcraft and territorial witchcraft, in the name of Jesus.

20. I set confusion, commotion, quarrels, misunderstanding and fighting in the camp of witchcraft powers, in the name of Jesus.

21. I sprinkle the overcoming and ever winning blood of Jesus in the camp of witches and wizards, in the name of Jesus.

22. I set ablaze with the fire of the Holy Spirit, every file, document and information that witches and wizards have on me and my family, in the name of Jesus.

23.I destroy perpetually, every monitoring gadget, telescope, cameras, radios, televisions, spiritual wires, witches and wizards have on me, in the name of Jesus.

24.I confess and repent in totality, every sin that gave the witches and wizards entrance into my life, in the name of Jesus.

25.It is written, touch not My anointed, and do My prophets no harm. I am the anointed of the Lord of salvation, and I neutralize evil activities in my life, in the name of Jesus.

26.I destroy all witchcraft terrors by night and all their arrows that fly by the day, in the name of Jesus.

27.It is written that 1,000 shall fall at my side and 10,000 at my right hand, but none shall come near me. Therefore, I command all witches assigned against my life to fall and never to rise again, in the name of Jesus.

28.I receive divine deliverance from every snare of the fowler and from the noisome pestilence organized by witches against me, in the name of Jesus.

29.I decree that the powers of witches shall not exact upon me, nor their wickedness afflict me, in the name of Jesus.

30.I call upon the Lord to plead my cause with them that strive against me, fight against them that fight against me, in the name of Jesus.

31. I command every witchcraft deposit made on my body while I slept to leave, in the name of Jesus.

32. I release my divine blessings which are locked up by witchcraft powers in the air, in the name of Jesus.

33. I release destruction against the witchcraft forces unawares, in the name of Jesus.

34. Every pit the witches have dug for me, without cause or reason, I decree all of them to fall into it, in the name of Jesus.

35. I blind the eyes of witches never to see me, I cause their ways to be dark and slippery and their very net to catch all of them, in the name of Jesus.

36. I turn the witches assigned against my life to be as the chaff before the wind of the Lord, I chase them out of my terrain, business, family and life, in the name of Jesus.

37. The rod of witchcraft wickedness, shall not rest upon me, my family and business for ever, in the name of Jesus.

38. The Lord shall preserve me from all evil, in my going out and in my coming in, in the name of Jesus.

39. As all the armies of Pharaoh perished in the Red Sea, so shall all witches and wizards pursuing me perish in their own Red Sea, in the name of Jesus.

40.Begin to thank God for the victory.

WARFARE NUMBER 6

BURY YOUR HAMAN

Confession:

Rev. 13:10: He that leadeth into captivity shall go into captivity: he that killeth with the sword must be killed with the sword. Here is the patience and the faith of the saints.

Praise Worship

Prayer Points

1. Thank the Lord for He is the only One that answers prayers.
2. Every Haman assigned against my life, fall down and die, in the name of Jesus.
3. Every messenger of death assigned against my life, go back to your sender, in the name of Jesus.
4. Every agent of death buried inside my body, come out and die, in the name of Jesus.
5. Every gate of death assigned to swallow me, swallow your owner, in the name of Jesus.
6. Every plantation of death, die, in the name of Jesus.
7. Every stronghold of death on my mind and imagination, be pulled down, in the name of Jesus.
8. By the resurrection of the Lord Jesus Christ, the power of death is broken upon my life, in the name of Jesus.
9. Every string of death, fashioned against my life, be

neutralized by the blood of Jesus.

10. Every certificate of untimely death, issued against my life, catch fire, in the name of Jesus.

11. I shall not die but live to declare the works of God, in the name of Jesus.

12. The number of my days shall be fulfilled, in the name of Jesus.

13. Every damaged organ in my body, be repaired by fire, in the name of Jesus.

14. My bones shall not be broken through accident, in the name of Jesus.

15. Every power that does not want to see me around, fall down and die, in the name of Jesus.

16. My soul shall not see corruption of death through sickness, accident or calamity, in the name of Jesus.

17. I drink the blood of Jesus, let the life in the blood of Jesus flow into every organ of my body, in the name of Jesus.

18. My blood, by the blood of Jesus, be inoculated and immunized against the invasion of death, in the name of Jesus.

19. I eat of the flesh of Jesus, and I receive life into my body, in the name of Jesus.

20. Every arrow of untimely death fashioned against my life, go

back to your senders, in the name of Jesus.

21. Every power digging a grave for me, enter therein, in the name of Jesus.

22. The vehicle of my transportation shall not become my coffin, in the name of Jesus.

23. I shall not journey into death, in the name of Jesus.

24. Every snare of death set up for my life, catch your owners, in the name of Jesus.

25. There shall be no sorrow of death in my family, in the name of Jesus.

26. Every shadow of death assigned against my life, scatter, in the name of Jesus.

27. Let the mark of the blood of Jesus wipe off every mark of death on my body, in the name of Jesus.

28. Every stronghold of untimely death fashioned against my life, be pulled down by fire, in the name of Jesus.

29. You wind of death, go back to your sender, in the name of Jesus.

30. Every spirit of depression and despair, die, in the name of Jesus.

31. Every wind of death, go back to your sender, in the name of Jesus.

32.Every satanic device to terminate my life, catch fire, in the name of Jesus.

33.Let the tokens of the liars to cut off my life be frustrated, in the name of Jesus.

34.Every pollution of death, in the organ of my body, die, in the name of Jesus.

35.Let my blood be transfused with the blood of Jesus.

36.Every poison and contamination in my blood, be flushed out, in the name of Jesus.

37.Every tree of untimely death in my family line, my life is not your candidate, die, in the name of Jesus.

38.Every evil hunter of my soul, turn back and die, in the name of Jesus.

39.By the power in the blood of Jesus, I subdue death, oppression and violence, in the name of Jesus.

40.Oh God, I thank You for giving me life to replace death.

WARFARE NUMBER 7

PRAYERS TO DEFEAT ANTI-CONCEPTION WITCHCRAFT

Praise worship

Confessions: Psalm 35:1-8: Plead my cause, Oh Lord, with them that strive with me: fight against them that fight against me. Take hold of shield and buckler, and stand up for mine help. Draw out also the spear, and stop the way against them that persecute me: say unto my soul, I am thy salvation. Let them be confounded and put to shame that seek after my soul: let them be turned back and brought to confusion that devise my hurt. Let them be as chaff before the wind: and let the angel of the Lord chase them. Let their way be dark and slippery: and let the angel of the Lord persecute them. For without cause have they hid for me their net in a pi, , which without cause they have digged for my soul. Let destruction come upon him at unawares; and let his net that he hath hid catch himself: into that very destruction let him tall.

1. Every witchcraft power hindering my fruitfulness, be arrested, in the name of Jesus.
2. According to the word of God in Exodus 23:25-26, I shall not be barren, in the name of Jesus.
3. Every evil power and satanic conspiracy against my conception, scatter, in the name of Jesus.
4. Everything that satan has set into motion to make me barren, scatter, in the name of Jesus.

5. Every satanic hand, against my ability to have children, be cut off, in the name of Jesus.
6. Every seed of witchcraft inside my reproductive organs, hindering my conception, come out, in the name of Jesus.
7. Every witchcraft power manipulating my menstrual circle, loose your hold, in the name of Jesus.
8. Every satanic heat in my womb and waist, die, by the blood of Jesus.
9. Witchcraft spirit of barrenness of my father's house, release me, in the name of Jesus.
10. Every witchcraft power, monitoring the success of my conception, be arrested, in the name of Jesus.
11. Every witchcraft spirit, assigned to prevent pregnancy in my life, die, in the name of Jesus.
12. Witchcraft spirit, assigned against the sperm count of my husband, loose your hold, in the name of Jesus.
13. Every witchcraft power, causing erection failure, weakness of my husband's organ and impotency, loose your hold, in the name of Jesus.
14. You witchcraft power in charge of watery sperm, loose your hold, in the name of Jesus.
15. Every evil vow of the evil powers of my father's house against

my child-bearing, be revoked by the blood of Jesus.

16. Every witchcraft power, responsible for miscarriage of pregnancies in my life, be arrested, in the name of Jesus.

17. Every record of my name in the register of childless couples, be wiped off by the blood of Jesus.

18. Every covenant of spiritual marriage, be cancelled by the blood of Jesus.

19. Every evil hold, of the spirit husband upon my life, break by the blood of Jesus.

20. Every remnant of the sperm of the spirit husband in my reproductive system, be flushed out by the blood of Jesus.

21. Every anti-conception curse from spiritual partner upon my life, be cancelled by the blood of Jesus.

22. Every demonic object moving around in my reproductive systems, come out now, in the name of Jesus.

23. Every witchcraft point of contact in my reproductive system, die, in the name of Jesus.

24. Every witchcraft curse, of barrenness upon my life, die, by the blood of Jesus.

25. Every curse of barrenness upon my life, as a result of past abortions, be cancelled by the blood of Jesus.

26. Every anti-conception curse placed upon my life by former

partners, be cancelled by the blood of Jesus.

27. Every ancestral witchcraft curse, of barrenness upon my life, loose your hold, in the name of Jesus.

28. Ancestral evil powers of my father's house, causing barrenness in my family line, my life is not your candidate, release my conception, in the name of Jesus.

29. Every concoction and charm I used in the past that is now hindering my child-bearing, I vomit them by fire, in the name of Jesus.

30. I release, my life, the success of my conception, my reproductive organs and my children from every power that operates in the air, water, sun, moon, stars, forests, stones and ground, in the name of Jesus.

31. Oh God, arise and deliver my marriage from the spirit of childlessness, in the name of Jesus.

32. I release my babies from every witchcraft cage, in the name of Jesus.

33. Every covenant of barrenness with any water spirit, break, by the blood of Jesus.

34. Every spirit, that is against childbearing in my family line, loose your hold, in the name of Jesus.

35. Every witchcraft hand, holding my reproductive system, loose

your hold, in the name of Jesus.

36. I renounce every spiritual home with all its associated properties, in the name of Jesus.

37. Every witchcraft cage, holding my womb, die, in the name of Jesus.

38. Every witchcraft cage, holding my marriage, die, in the name of Jesus.

39. Every witchcraft blanket, holding my children, die, in the name of Jesus.

40. Every witchcraft gate, barricade and checkpoint, set up against my marriage, scatter, in the name of Jesus.

41. Every witchcraft chain of stagnancy, holding me to one spot, break and die, in the name of Jesus.

42. Every witchcraft dominion over my life as a result of my past encounter with any native doctor, scatter, in the name of Jesus.

43. Every witchcraft altar, raised against my conception, be pulled down, in the name of Jesus.

44. Every witchcraft cobweb, upon my life, burn to ashes by the fire of God, in the name of Jesus.

45. Every witchcraft burial, against my marriage, die, in the name of Jesus.

46. Every witchcraft burial, against my conception, die, in the name of Jesus.

47. Every witchcraft summon, to manipulate my conception, scatter, in the name of Jesus.

48. Every witchcraft case file, on my marriage and conception, catch fire, in the name of Jesus.

49. Every witchcraft coven, set up against my marriage and conception, die, in the name of Jesus.

50. Every witchcraft gun-shot in the dream, backfire, in the name of Jesus.

51. Every witchcraft injection in the dream, die, in the name of Jesus.

52. Every witchcraft food in the dream, die, in the name of Jesus.

53. Every witchcraft attack in the dream, die, in the name of Jesus.

54. Every witchcraft family altar, catch fire, in the name of Jesus.

55. You witchcraft strongman in my family line, loose your hold upon my life, in the name of Jesus.

56. Every witchcraft cellophane, covering my womb, catch fire, in the name of Jesus.

57. Every witchcraft kingdom, in my family line, be overthrown by

fire, in the name of Jesus.

58. I release my marriage and conception, from the dominion of witchcraft powers, in the name of Jesus.

59. Every witchcraft pot, prepared for me and my family, catch fire, in the name of Jesus.

60. Every witchcraft hand, feeding my babies in the womb, be cut off, in the name of Jesus.

61. Every witchcraft deposit, in my reproductive organs, be flushed out by the blood of Jesus.

62. Every witchcraft injection, in my reproductive organs, be flushed out by the blood of Jesus.

63. Every sexual witchcraft deposit, in my body, be flushed out by the blood of Jesus.

64. Every witchcraft tree, carrying the fruit of my womb, catch fire, in the name of Jesus.

65. Every witchcraft mark of failure, upon my life, be wiped off by the blood of Jesus.

66. Every witchcraft desire, for my marriage, die, in the name of Jesus.

67. Every witchcraft incantation and divination against my marriage and conception, die, in the name of Jesus.

68. Every witchcraft power, using the weapon of the dust against

my marriage and conception, die, in the name of Jesus.

69. Every witchcraft-induced sickness preventing my conception, die, in the name of Jesus.

70. Oh Lord, let my life become a no-go-area for witchcraft powers in the dream, in the name of Jesus.

71. Every witchcraft stronghold, causing barrenness in my marriage, be pulled down by fire, in the name of Jesus.

72. Any power, spirit or personality, that has entered into witchcraft covenants against my life, scatter, in the name of Jesus.

73. Every power, spirit and personality, that has entered into witchcraft covenants against my conception, scatter, in the name of Jesus.

74. Every witchcraft monitoring gadget, set up against the success of my conception, catch fire, in the name of Jesus.

75. Every witchcraft foundation, in the foundation of my life, catch fire and die, in the name of Jesus.

76. Blood of Jesus, blot out every witchcraft handwriting and ordinances that are working against my life in the heavenlies, in the name of Jesus.

77. Every witchcraft time, agenda and calendar for my life, catch fire, in the name of Jesus.

78.Every evil power monitoring the progress of evil in my family line, be arrested, in the name of Jesus.

79.By the blood of Jesus, let evil seasons in my family line stop, in the name of Jesus.

80.Every witchcraft altar ministering barrenness into my marriage, scatter, in the name of Jesus.

81. Let confusion, baptise the camp of witchcraft powers, assigned against my life, in the name of Jesus.

82.Every witchcraft-induced tongue, speaking evil into my marriage, die, in the name of Jesus.

83.Let the dwelling place of witchcraft powers, in my family line, become desolate by the blood of Jesus.

84.You heavens, rain snares, fire and brimstone on the witchcraft powers that are depriving me of conception, in the name of Jesus.

85.By the blood of Jesus, let every witchcraft association against my marriage scatter, in the name of Jesus.

86.Every evil word, by witchcraft powers against my life, fall to the ground and die, in the name of Jesus.

87.Every witchcraft horn raised against my life, be cut off, in the name of Jesus.

88.Every evil flow of ancestral witchcraft powers into my life, dry up, in the name of Jesus.

89. Oh God, arise and scatter every witchcraft judgement, against my life, in the name of Jesus.

90. Begin to thank God for answers to your prayers.

WARFARE NUMBER 8

WITCHCRAFT MUST DIE

Praise Worship

Confessions

Exodus 22:18: Thou shalt not suffer a witch to live.

Rev. 12:11: And they overcame him by the blood of the Lamb, and by the word of their testimony; and they loved not their lives unto the death.

Prayer warfare

1. O Rock of Ages, smash into pieces every foundation of witchcraft in my family, in the name of Jesus. Thou foundation of witchcraft in my father's house / mother's house, die, in the name of Jesus.
2. Let witchcraft powers eat their own flesh and drink their own blood, in the name of Jesus.
3. Every seat of witchcraft, receive the thunder fire of God, in the name of Jesus.
4. Let the habitation of witchcraft powers, be desolate, in the name of Jesus.
5. Every throne of witchcraft, be dismantled by fire, in Jesus' name.
6. Let the stronghold of witchcraft powers, be pulled down by fire, in the name of Jesus.
7. Let the refuge of witchcraft, be disgraced, in Jesus' name.

8. Let the network of witchcraft, disintegrate, in Jesus' name.
9. Let the communication systems of witchcraft powers, be destroyed by fire, in the name of Jesus.
10. Every transportation system of witchcraft powers, be disrupted, in the name of Jesus.
11. Let the weapons of witchcraft powers, turn against them, in the name of Jesus.
12. I withdraw my blessings from every bank or strongroom of the enemy, in the name of Jesus.
13. Oh altar of witchcraft, break, in the name of Jesus.
14. Every witchcraft padlock fashioned against me, break by fire, in the name of Jesus.
15. Every trap of witchcraft, catch your owners, in Jesus' name.
16. Every witchcraft utterance and projection made against me, be overthrown, in the name of Jesus.
17. I reverse every witchcraft burial, fashioned against me, in the name of Jesus.
18. I deliver my soul from every witchcraft bewitchment, in the name of Jesus.
19. I reverse the effect of every witchcraft summoning of my spirit, in the name of Jesus.

20. Every witchcraft identification mark, be wiped off by the blood of Jesus.

21. I frustrate every witchcraft exchange of my virtues, in the name of Jesus.

22. Let the blood of Jesus block, the flying route, of witchcraft powers targeted against me.

23. Let every witchcraft curse, break and be destroyed, in Jesus' name.

24. Every covenant of witchcraft, melt, by the blood of Jesus.

25. I withdraw every organ of my body, from any witchcraft altar, in the name of Jesus.

26. Anything planted in my life by witchcraft, come out now and die, in the name of Jesus.

27. Let the blood of Jesus cancel every witchcraft initiation, fashioned against my destiny, in the name of Jesus.

28. Every witchcraft poison, be destroyed, in the name of Jesus.

29. I reverse every witchcraft pattern, fashioned against my destiny, in the name of Jesus.

30. Every witchcraft cage, fashioned against my life, be destroyed, in the name of Jesus.

31. Let every problem in my life that originated from witchcraft, receive divine instant solution, in Jesus' name.

32.I command all the damages done to my life by witchcraft to be repaired, in the name of Jesus.

33.Let every blessing, confiscated by witchcraft spirits, be released, in Jesus' name.

34.Every witchcraft power assigned against my life and marriage, receive . . . (pick from the under- listed), in Jesus' name.

- the thunder and lightning of God
- hail and fire mingled with the blood of the Lamb
- unbearable heat
- concentrated acid
- destroying flood
- destruction
- raging fire
- continuous plagues
- failure
- confusion

35.I loose myself, from any power of witchcraft, in Jesus' name.

36.Every camp of witchcraft, gathered against my prosperity, fall down and die, in Jesus' name.

37.Every witchcraft pot, working against me, I bring the judgment of God against you, in the name of Jesus.

38. I command every witchcraft pot, using remote control against my health, to be broken into pieces, in Jesus' name.

39. Witchcraft opposition, receive the rain of affliction, in the name of Jesus.

40. Let the spirit of witchcraft, attack the familiar spirits, fashioned against me, in Jesus' name.

41. I retrieve my integrity, out of the hands of household witchcraft, in the name of Jesus.

42. I break the power of the occult, witchcraft and familiar spirits over my life, in Jesus' name.

43. In the name of Jesus, I break and loose myself from all evil curses, chains, spells, jinx, bewitchments, witchcraft or sorcery which may have been put upon me.

44. Let the thunder of God, locate and dismantle the throne of witchcraft in my household, in the name of Jesus.

45. Let every seat of witchcraft, in my household, be roasted by the fire of God, in Jesus' name.

46. Let the altar of witchcraft, in my household, be roasted, in the name of Jesus.

47. Let the thunder of God, scatter beyond redemption, the foundation of witchcraft in my household, in Jesus' name.

48. Every stronghold of refuge, of my household witches, be

destroyed, in the name of Jesus.

49. Every hiding and secret places of witchcraft in my family, be exposed by fire, in the name of Jesus.

50. Let every local and international witchcraft network, of my household witches, be shattered into pieces, in Jesus' name.

51. Let the communication system, of my household witches, be frustrated, in the name of Jesus.

52. Let the terrible fire of God, consume the transportation of my household witchcraft, in the name of Jesus.

53. Every agent, ministering at the altar of witchcraft in my household, fall down and die, in the name of Jesus.

54. Let the thunder and the fire of God, locate the storehouses and strongrooms of the household witchcraft harbouring my blessings, and pull them down, in the name of Jesus.

55. Let any witchcraft curse, working against me, be revoked by the blood of Jesus.

56. Every decision, vow and covenant of household witchcraft affecting me, be nullified by the blood of Jesus.

57. I destroy with the fire of God, every weapon of witchcraft used against me, in Jesus' name.

58. Any material taken from my body and now placed on a witchcraft altar, be roasted by the fire of God, in Jesus'

name.

59.I reverse every witchcraft burial fashioned against me, in the name of Jesus.

60.Every trap set for me by witches, begin to catch your owners, in the name of Jesus.

61. Every witchcraft padlock, fashioned against any area of my life, be roasted, in Jesus' name.

62.Let the wisdom of household witches be converted to foolishness, in the name of Jesus.

63.Let the wickedness of household enemies, overtake them, in the name of Jesus.

64.I deliver my soul from every witchcraft bewitchment, in the name of Jesus.

65.Any witchcraft bird flying for my sake, fall down, die and be roasted to ashes, in the name of Jesus.

66.Any of my blessings traded with by household witches, be returned to me, in Jesus' name.

67.Any of my blessings and testimonies swallowed by witches, be converted to hot coals of fire of God and be vomited, in the name of Jesus.

68.I break myself loose, from every bondage of witchcraft covenants, in the name of Jesus.

69. Any witchcraft coven, where any of my blessings are hidden, be roasted by the fire of God, in the name of Jesus.

70. (Lay your right hand on your head) Every witchcraft spirit plantation, pollution, deposit and material in my body, melt by the fire of God and be flushed out by the blood of Jesus.

71. Every evil, ever done to me through witchcraft attack, be reversed, in the name of Jesus.

72. Every witchcraft hand planting evil seeds in my life through attacks in the dream, wither and burn to ashes, in Jesus' name.

73. Every witchcraft obstacle, put on the road to my desired miracle and success, be removed by the east wind of God, in Jesus' name.

74. Every witchcraft chant, spell and projection made against me, I bind you and turn you against your owner, in Jesus' name.

75. I frustrate every plot, device, scheme and project of witchcraft designed to affect any area of my life, in the name of Jesus.

76. Any witch projecting himself into the body of any animal in order to do me harm, be trapped in the body of such an animal forever, in the name of Jesus.

77. Any drop of my blood sucked by any witch, be vomited now, in

the name of Jesus.

78. Any part of me shared out amongst household/village witches, I recover you, in the name of Jesus.

79. Any organ of my body that has been exchanged for another through witchcraft operation, be replaced now, in Jesus' name.

80. I recover any of my virtues/blessings shared out amongst village / household witches, in the name of Jesus.

81. I reverse the evil effect of any witchcraft invocation or summoning of my spirit, in the name of Jesus.

82. I loose my hands and feet from any witchcraft bewitchment or bondage, in Jesus' name.

83. Let the blood of Jesus, wash away every witchcraft identification mark on me or on any of my properties, in Jesus' name.

84. I forbid any re-union or re-gathering of household and village witches against my life, in the name of Jesus.

85. Let the entire body system of my household witches begin to run amok until they confess all their wickedness, in Jesus' name.

86. Let the mercy of God be withdrawn from them, in Jesus' name.

87. Let them begin to grope in the daytime as in the thickness of

a dark night, in the name of Jesus.

88.Let everything that has ever worked for them begin to work against them, in Jesus' name.

89.Let them not have a cloth to cover their shame, in Jesus' name.

90.Let as many of them that are stubbornly unrepentant, be smitten by the sun in the day and by the moon in the night, in Jesus' name.

91. Let each step they take lead them to greater destruction, in the name of Jesus.

92.But as for me, let me dwell in the hollow of God's hand, in the name of Jesus.

93.Let the goodness and mercy of God overwhelm me now, in the name of Jesus.

94.Any witchcraft operation under any water against my life, receive immediate judgment of fire, in the name of Jesus.

95.Every witchcraft power, that has introduced spirit husband/wife or child into my dreams, be roasted by fire, in the name of Jesus.

96.Every agent of witchcraft power, posing as my husband/wife or child in my dreams, be roasted by fire, in Jesus' name.

97.Every agent of witchcraft power, physically attached to my marriage to frustrate it, fall down now and perish, in Jesus' name.

98. Every agent of witchcraft power, assigned to attack my finances through the dream, fall down and perish, in Jesus' name.

99. Let the thunderbolts of God, locate and destroy every witchcraft power coven, where deliberations and decisions were fashioned against me, in the name of Jesus.

100. Any water spirit, from my village or place of birth, practising witchcraft against me and my family, be amputated by the Word of God, in the name of Jesus.

101. Any power of witchcraft, holding any of my blessings in bondage, receive the fire of God and release them, in the name of Jesus.

102. I loose my mind and soul from the bondage of marine witches, in the name of Jesus.

103. Any witchcraft power chain, binding my hands and feet from prospering, be shattered into pieces, in Jesus' name.

104. Every arrow shot into my life from under any water through witchcraft, come out of me and go back to your sender, in the name of Jesus.

105. Any evil material, transferred into my body, through

contact with any witchcraft agent, roast by fire, in the name of Jesus.

106. Any evil done against me, through witchcraft oppression or manipulation, be reversed by the blood of Jesus.

107. I bind every witchcraft control and mind-blinding spirit, in the name of Jesus.

108. I cast out every witchcraft arrow affecting my senses (sight, smell, taste, hearing), in the name of Jesus.

109. I command every witchcraft arrow to depart from my ___, in the name of Jesus.

- spinal cord - spleen - navel - heart
- throat - eyes -head

110. Let the blood of Jesus, purge me of every witchcraft contaminating material, in the name of Jesus.

111. I destroy, the hand of any witch-doctor, working against me, in the name of Jesus.

112. Every witchcraft spirit, attempting to build a wall against my destiny, fall down and die, in the name of Jesus.

113. I send the rain of affliction upon every witchcraft power working against me, in the name of Jesus.

114. Oh sun, moon, stars, earth, water and the elements, vomit every enchantment that is against me, in the name of

Jesus

115. Every power using the heavenlies against me, fall down and be disgraced, in Jesus' name.

116. Let the stars of heaven begin to fight for me, in Jesus' name.

117. Oh God, arise and scatter every conspiracy in the heavenlies that is against me, in Jesus' name.

118. I break with the blood of Jesus all evil soul-ties affecting my life, in the name of Jesus.

119. Spirit of the living God, come upon my life and place a shield of protection around me, in the name of Jesus.

120. Every chain of inherited witchcraft in my family, break, in the name of Jesus.

121. Every ladder, used by witchcraft against me, be roasted, in the name of Jesus.

122. Any door, that I have opened to witchcraft in any area of my life, be closed for ever by the blood of Jesus.

123. I revoke every witchcraft verdict on my marital life, in the name of Jesus.

124. I send confusion into the camp of household witchcraft, in the name of Jesus.

125. Stubborn witchcraft, release me, in the name of Jesus.

126. Every witchcraft power working against my destiny, fall down and die, in Jesus' name.

127. Every incantation, ritual and witchcraft power against my destiny, fall down and die, in the name of Jesus.

128. I break the power of the occult, witchcraft and familiar spirits over my life, in Jesus' name.

129. Witchcraft opposition, receive the rain of affliction, in the name of Jesus.

130. I cancel, every witchcraft verdict, against my life, in Jesus' name.

131. I command every arrow of witchcraft in my life: Come out with all your roots, in the name of Jesus! (Lay your hands on your stomach and pray aggressively.)

132. I command every witchcraft pot, using remote control against my health, to be broken into pieces, in Jesus' name.

133. I rebuke the spell of any witchcraft pot from my neck, in the name of Jesus.

134. I break every witchcraft pot over my life, in Jesus' name.

135. Every council of witchcraft working against me will not prosper, in the name of Jesus.

136. I release myself and my family from every witchcraft cage and pot, in the name of Jesus.

137. I retrieve my integrity from the hands of household witchcraft, in the name of Jesus.

138. Every witchcraft hand, planting evil seeds in my life through attacks in the dream, wither and burn to ashes, in Jesus' name.

139. Let all friendly witchcraft powers be exposed and disgraced, in the name of Jesus.

140. Oh Lord, plant Your warring angels around me, to dismantle and destroy evil stronghold of internal witchcraft.

141. I exercise my authority, over stubborn witchcraft and I pull down its structures, in Jesus' name.

142. Every placenta witchcraft, targeted against my destiny, what are you waiting for? die, in the name of Jesus.

143. Placenta witchcraft, manipulating my destiny, die, in Jesus' name

144. Every blessing, that I have lost through placenta witchcraft, I repossess you, in Jesus' name.

145. Every witchcraft coven and marine bank, release my placenta, in Jesus' name

146. Every cage of family witchcraft, release my divine partner, in Jesus' name.

147. Oh Lord, let my dreams and visions, reject every

witchcraft projection, in the name of Jesus.

148. Thank God for answers to your prayers.

WARFARE NUMBER 9

DISGRACING THE WICKED

CONFESSION

2 Samuel 2:6-10; Isaiah 7:7-11

Praise worship

1. I render every altar of aggression impotent, in the name of Jesus.
2. Every evil altar erected against me, be disgraced, in the name of Jesus.
3. Anything done against my life under demonic anointing, be nullified, in the name of Jesus.
4. I curse every local altar fashioned against me, in the name of Jesus.
5. Let the hammer of the Almighty God, smash every evil altar erected against me, in the name of Jesus.
6. Oh Lord, send Your fire, to destroy every evil altar fashioned against me, in the name of Jesus.
7. Every evil priest, ministering against me at the evil altar, receive the sword of God, in the name of Jesus.
8. Let the thunder of God, smite every evil priest working against me on the evil altar and burn them to ashes, in the name of Jesus.
9. Let every satanic priest, ministering against me at evil altars fall down and die, in the name of Jesus.

10. Any hand, that wants to retaliate or arrest me because of all these prayers I am praying, dry up and wither, in the name of Jesus.
11. Every stubborn evil altar priest, drink your own blood, in the name of Jesus.
12. I possess my possession, stolen by the evil altar, in the name of Jesus.
13. I withdraw my name, from every evil altar, in the name of Jesus.
14. I withdraw my blessings, from every evil altar, in the name of Jesus.
15. I withdraw my breakthroughs, from every evil altar, in the name of Jesus.
16. I withdraw my glory, from every evil altar, in the name of Jesus.
17. I withdraw my prosperity, from every evil altar, in the name of Jesus.
18. I withdraw anything representing me, from every evil altar, in the name of Jesus.
19. Mention the organ that you know is not behaving the way it should. When you have done this, begin to say, I withdraw you from every evil altar, in the name of Jesus. Say this seven hot

times.

20.Let the wind of the Holy Spirit bring every scattered bone together now, in the name of Jesus.

21. I use the blood of Jesus to reverse every poor record of the past about my life, in the name of Jesus.

22.I refuse to accept, satanic substitute for my destiny, in the name of Jesus.

23.I refuse to be caged, by the enemy of good things, in the name of Jesus.

24.Let every internal coffin in my life, receive the fire of God and be roasted now, in the name of Jesus.

25.Every destiny-paralysing power, fashioned against my destiny, fall down and die, in the name of Jesus.

26.Every inherited evil limitation, in any area of my life, depart now, in the name of Jesus.

27.Every architect of spiritual coffins, I command you to fall down and die, in the name of Jesus.

28.Every cloud of uncertainty, clear away now, in the name of Jesus.

29.I refuse to be converted to a living dead, in the name of Jesus.

30.Let every evil laying-on of hands and shaking of evil hands be nullified, in the name of Jesus.

31. Every satanic consultation, concerning my life, be nullified, in the name of Jesus.

32. Every decision, taken against my life by witchcraft spirits, be nullified, in the name of Jesus.

33. I reject, aborted victories in every area of my life, in the name of Jesus.

34. Every caged star, be released now, in the name of Jesus.

35. My imagination and dreams will not be used against me, in the name of Jesus.

36. Oh God, arise and visit all shrines assigned against me with thunder and earthquake, in the name of Jesus.

37. All satanic altars, erected against my destiny, be overthrown by fire, in the name of Jesus.

38. Oh God, arise and set unquenchable fire, upon every coven of darkness assigned against me, in the name of Jesus.

39. All images, carved against my life, break into pieces after the order of dagon, in the name of Jesus.

40. Oh God, arise and cause confusion in the camp of my enemies, in the name of Jesus.

41. I decree that my oppressors shall consult their powers in their confusion, but there will be no response, in the name of

Jesus.

42.Holy Ghost fire, arise and stir up civil war in the camp of my enemies, in the name of Jesus.

43.I command every satanic intermediary, working against me, to loose heart, in the name of Jesus.

44.Oh God, arise and bring the plans of my oppressors to nothing, in the name of Jesus.

45.My Father, set up a fierce king against my oppressors and let the king treat them with great torture, in the name of Jesus.

46.Let the power of God, intimidate and frustrate all diviners assigned against me, in the name of Jesus.

47.Oh God, arise and wipe out the understanding of my stubborn pursuers, in the name of Jesus.

48.Oh God, pour out the spirit of dizziness upon all evil spiritual consultants speaking against me, in the name of Jesus.

49.Let these evil spiritual consultants, stagger in all they do as a drunkard staggers in his vomit, in thc name of Jesus,

50.By the power in the blood of Jesus, let all soothsayers, witchdoctors, enchanters arranged against me be cut off, in the name of Jesus.

51. Oh heavens, Oh earth, hear the word of the Lord: you must not execute the counsel of my enemies, in the name of Jesus.

52. Oh God, pass through the camp of my enemies with affliction, and drain the anointing of wickedness, in the name of Jesus.

53. Every power assigned to wreck my destiny, your end has come, die, in the name of Jesus.

54. I de-programme and cancel all negative prophecies pronounced against me, in the name of Jesus.

55. Oh Lord, guide me into the mysteries of my life, in Jesus' name.

56. Oh Lord, give me the keys, to unlock the hidden riches of secret places, in the name of Jesus.

57. All ancient doors, that have hindered the plan of God for my life, be unlocked by fire, in the name of Jesus.

58. I destroy every agreement, made at covens and satanic centres against me, in the name of Jesus.

59. Every secret code, evil registers and archives of the enemy in my place of birth, be roasted, in the name of Jesus.

60. Oh God, arise and cast abominable filth upon witches and wizards and set them as gazing stock, in the name of Jesus.

61. Let the tables of witches and wizards become snares unto them, in the name of Jesus.

62. Let the eyes of witches monitoring my life go blind, in the name of Jesus.

63.Let the covens of witchcraft, become desolate, let there be no one to dwell in them, in the name of Jesus.

64.I command crashlanding of witches and wizards assigned against my breakthrough, in the name of Jesus.

65.I command the sun to smite my oppressors in the day and the moon and the stars to smite them at night, in the name of Jesus.

66.I command the stars in their courses to fight against my stubborn pursuers, in the name of Jesus.

67.Oh God, arise, roar and prevail over my enemies, in the name of Jesus.

68.Let the gathering of the wicked, against me, be harvested for judgement, in the name of Jesus.

69.Oh God, arise and hang every Haman assigned against my life, in the name of Jesus.

70.Every stumbling block, to God's prophetic agenda for my life, be rooted out, in the name of Jesus.

71. All negative words, that have been spoken against me by evil men, die, in the name of Jesus.

72.All evil records, evil marriage certificates and registers that are kept in satanic archives against me, be wiped off by the blood of Jesus.

73.I programme divine health, divine favour, long life, spiritual advancement into my life by the power in the blood of Jesus.

74.I close down, every spiritual ship, carting away my benefits, in the name of Jesus.

75.Oh God, arise and lay waste, all the operations of dark forces, working against me, in the name of Jesus.

WARFARE NUMBER 10

POWER AGAINST WITCHCRAFT FORCES

Praise worship

Confessions:

In the name of Jesus, I believe the word of God is steadfast, and unshakeable, endures forever and is powerful. It is the power of God that is able to deliver me out of any bondage.

The word of God is God Himself speaking and not man. Therefore, nothing shall be impossible for me because of the word of God which I believe in my heart and confess with my mouth.

Father Lord, as I make this confession now, I pray that You will watch over Your word to perform it, because You are a faithful God. You are not a man that You should lie, neither the son of man that You should repent. Rather You will not break Your covenant, nor alter the word which has gone forth out of Your mouth.

It is written, when I ask, I should believe and receive. As I make this confession and go into prayer, I will receive, according to the word of God, dominion and power, because I know God will prove Himself strong on my behalf, for my heart is focused on Him.

I know who I am in Christ. I have been purchased by the blood of Jesus Christ that was shed for me on the cross of Calvary. I am a child of God. I am called by the name of the Lord. I am bought by the blood of the Lamb of God. I believe the power in the blood of Jesus. Jesus has translated my life from the kingdom of darkness into His own marvelous kingdom of light and peace. I now belong to the kingdom of God. I have the keys of the kingdom of God in my hands to bind and to loose. I have the authority to trample under my feet, serpents, scorpions and all the powesr of the enemy.

Jesus Christ, through His death, has destroyed satan, who had the power of death. Jesus has delivered my life from death and damnation. Before Jesus ascended, He first of all descended into the lower parts of the earth and stripped the devil of all his power over me. Jesus has taken from satan the keys of death and hell and has given them to me to bind and to loose.

By virtue of the work Jesus Christ did on the cross, I have power over all the power of the enemy. He has wiped out all the handwriting of requirements that were against me, took them out of the way, having nailed them to the cross. He disarmed principalities and powers and made a show of them openly, triumphing over them in it.

I hold in my hand now the victory won for me by my Saviour, Jesus Christ on the cross of Calvary and I say, be shattered O you witches and powers of wickedness and be broken into pieces. Give ear all you powers of wickedness from my place of birth or origin, gird yourselves and you shall be broken into pieces. Take your counsel together and it will come to nothing. Chant your incantations, they will not stand, for the Lord is with me as a mighty and terrible one. Therefore, you shall stumble and fall.

Encamp against me, but my heart shall not fear, for in the name of the Lord, I will destroy you. The Lord is the strength of my life, of whom shall I be afraid. Surround me like bees and I will quench you all, like a fire of thorns.

Fashion your weapons of wickedness, and they will not prosper. Rise up against me in judgement with all your legal grounds and you shall all be condemned because that is my heritage as a servant of God.

I shall not die but live. Any power that has ever led me captive shall go into captivity. They that afflict and oppress me shall be ashamed. God will contend with all who contend with me. He will feed those who oppress me with their own flesh and they shall be drunk with their own blood as with sweet wine, for the Lord will bring upon them the day of the doom and destroy them with double destruction.

It is written that God will light my lamp and enlighten my darkness. But every satanic agent or power oppressing me shall grope in the day time as in thick blackness and darkness.

It is written that I shall be strong in the Lord and in the power of His might, therefore I ask that as I go into prayer right now the Lord will be my strength; the strength to run through a troop, to leap over any wall, to pursue and overtake my enemies, to recover my stolen properties, to beat them as small as the dust, to withstand and overcome all spiritual oppositions and distractions.

I hold in my hand the shield of faith for it is written that whosoever is born of God overcometh the world. And this is the victory that overcometh the world and its wickedness, even my faith.

In faith I go into this prayer session. In faith I have the victory. In faith my enemies are all subdued under my feet and none shall be able to escape.

My heart steadfastly believes the word of God. I have confessed with my mouth and by the word of my mouth let me be justified Oh Lord, and let all my enemies be condemned. I seal my confession with the blood of Jesus. (Amen.)

1. Let the thunder of God, locate and dismantle the throne of witchcraft in my household, in the name of Jesus.
2. Let every seat of witchcraft in my household, be roasted with the fire of God, in the name of Jesus.
3. Let the altar of witchcraft in my household, be roasted, in the name of Jesus.
4. Let the thunder of God, scatter beyond redemption the foundation of witchcraft in my household, in Jesus' name.

5. Every stronghold or refuge of my household witches, be destroyed, in the name of Jesus.
6. Every hiding and secret places of witchcraft in my family, be exposed by fire, in the name of Jesus.
7. Let every local and international witchcraft network, of my household witches, be shattered into pieces, in Jesus' name.
8. Let the communication system, of my household witches, be frustrated, in the name of Jesus.
9. Let the terrible fire of God, consume the transportation of my household witchcraft, in the name of Jesus.
10. Every agent, ministering at the altar of witchcraft, in my household, fall down and die, in the name of Jesus.
11. Let the thunder and the fire of God locate the storehouses and strongrooms of my household witchcraft harbouring my blessings and pull them down, in the name of Jesus.
12. Let any witchcraft curse, working against, me be revoked by the blood of Jesus.
13. Every decision, vow and covenant of household witchcraft affecting me, be nullified by the blood of Jesus.
14. I destroy with the fire of God, every weapon of witchcraft used against me, in the name of Jesus.
15. Any material taken from my body, and placed on witchcraft

altar, be roasted by the fire of God, in the name of Jesus.

16. I reverse, every witchcraft burial, fashioned against me, in the name of Jesus.

17. Every trap, set for me by witches, begin to catch your owners, in the name of Jesus.

18. Every witchcraft padlock, fashioned against any area of my life be roasted, in the name of Jesus.

19. Let the wisdom of my household witches be converted to foolishness, in the name of Jesus.

20. Let the wickedness of my household enemies overturn them, in the name of Jesus.

21. I deliver my soul from every witchcraft bewitchment, in the name of Jesus.

22. Any witchcraft bird, flying for my sake, fall down and die and be roasted to ashes, in the name of Jesus.

23. Any of my blessing, traded out by household witches be returned to me, in the name of Jesus.

24. Any of my blessings and testimonies swallowed by witches, be converted to hot coals of fire of God and be vomited, in the name of Jesus.

25. I break myself loose, from every bondage of witchcraft covenant, in the name of Jesus.

26.Any witchcraft coven where any of my blessings are hidden, be roasted by the fire of God, in Jesus' name.

27.(Lay your right hand on your head) Every witchcraft spirit plantation, pollution, deposits and materials in my body, be melted by the fire of God and be flushed out by the blood of Jesus.

28.Every evil ever done to me, through witchcraft attack, be reversed, in the name of Jesus.

29.Every damage done to my destiny, through witchcraft operations, be reversed now, in the name of Jesus.

30.Every witchcraft hand, planting evil seeds in my life through attacks in my dream, wither and burn to ashes, in the name of Jesus.

31. Every witchcraft obstacle and hindrance put on the road to my desired miracle and success, be removed by the east wind of God, in the name of Jesus.

32.Every witchcraft chants, spells and projections made against me, I bind you and turn you against your owner, in the name of Jesus.

33.I frustrate every plot, device, scheme and projects of witchcraft designed to affect any area of my life, in the name of Jesus.

34. Any witch projecting into the blood of any animal in order to do me harm or evil, be trapped in the body of such an animal forever, in the name of Jesus.

35. Any drop of my blood sucked by any witch, be vomited now, in the name of Jesus.

36. Any part of me shared out amongst household / village witches, I recover you, in the name of Jesus.

37. Any organ of my body, that has been exchanged for another one through witchcraft operations, be replaced now, in the name of Jesus.

38. I recover any of my virtues / blessings shared out amongst village / household witches, in Jesus' name.

39. I reverse the evil effect of any witchcraft invocation or summoning of my spirit, in the name of Jesus.

40. I loose my hands and feet from any witchcraft bewitchment and bondage, in the name of Jesus.

41. Let the blood of Jesus wash away every witchcraft identification mark on me or on any of my property, in Jesus' name.

42. I forbid any re-union or re-gathering of household and village witches against my life, in the name of Jesus.

43. Let the entire body system of my household witches be upset

until they confess all their wickedness, in the name of Jesus.

As regards the household witches that are contrary to me:

44.Let the mercies of God be withdrawn from them, in Jesus' name.

45.Let them begin to grope in the daytime as in the thickness of a dark night, in the name of Jesus.

46.Let everything that has ever worked for them begin to work against them, in the name of Jesus.

47.Let them not have a cloth to cover their shame, in Jesus' name.

48.Let as many of them as are stubbornly unrepentant be smitten by the sun in the day and by the moon at night, in the name of Jesus.

49.Let each step they take lead them to greater destruction, in the name of Jesus.

50.But as for me, let me dwell in the hollow of God's hand, in the name of Jesus.

51. Let the goodness and mercy of God now overwhelm me, in the name of Jesus.

52.I force-feed witchcraft powers with their own blood, in the name of Jesus.

53.Every foundation of witchcraft in my household, be smashed by the Rock of ages, in the name of Jesus.

54. Every seat of witchcraft, receive the thunder fire of God, in the name of Jesus.

55. Every habitation of witchcraft, be scattered unto desolation, in the name of Jesus.

56. Every throne of witchcraft, be dismantled by fire, in the name of Jesus.

57. Every stronghold of witchcraft in my life, receive divine acid, in the name of Jesus.

58. Let the witchcraft network be shattered into pieces, in the name of Jesus.

59. Let their communication system be damaged by fire, in the name of Jesus.

60. Every stubborn and unrepentant witchcraft, be exposed and disgraced, in the name of Jesus.

61. Let their hiding places be consumed by fire, in Jesus' name.

62. Let their transportation system scatter into pieces, in the name of Jesus.

63. I withdraw my blessings from every witchcraft storehouse and strongroom, in the name of Jesus.

64. Let every witchcraft curse, go back to the sender, seven fold, in the name of Jesus.

65. Every covenant of witchcraft, be melted by the blood of Jesus.

66. Every weapon of witchcraft, turn against your users, in the name of Jesus.

67. I reverse every witchcraft burial, fashioned against me, in the name of Jesus.

68. I withdraw every organ of my body, from any witchcraft altar, in the name of Jesus.

69. Every trap of witchcraft, catch your owner, in the name of Jesus.

70. Every witchcraft padlock, fashioned against me, be roasted, in the name of Jesus.

71. I deliver my soul, from every witchcraft bewitchment, in the name of Jesus.

72. Every damage done to my destiny by witchcraft, be reversed, in the name of Jesus.

73. Every witchcraft utterance and projections made against me, be overthrown, in the name of Jesus.

74. Any drop of my blood sucked by any witch, be vomitted now, in the name of Jesus.

75. I reverse the effect of every witchcraft summoning of my spirit, in the name of Jesus.

76.Every witchcraft identification mark, be wiped off by the blood of Jesus.

77.I frustrate every witchcraft exchange of my virtues, in the name of Jesus.

78.Anything planted in my life by witchcraft, come out now, in the name of Jesus.

79.Let each step taken by witchcraft against me lead them to their own greater destruction, in the name of Jesus.

80.I declare my environment and my house a no-flying zone for witchcraft birds, in the name of Jesus.

81. I cut off the roots of witchcraft in the water, in the name of Jesus.

82.Anything, deposited in my life, by marine witchcraft, come out now, in the name of Jesus.

83.Anything, deposited in my life, by household witchcraft, come out now, in the name of Jesus.

WARFARE NUMBER 11

DESTRUCTION OF EVIL CALDRONS (POT)

Praise and Worship

Confession Ezek. 11:3,7; Which says, It is not near; let us build houses: this city is the caldron, and we be the flesh. . . Therefore thus saith the Lord GOD; Your slain whom ye have laid in the midst of it, they are the flesh, and this city is the caldron: but I will bring you forth out of the midst of it.

Micah 3:3: Who also eat the flesh of my people, and flay their skin from off them; and they break their bones, and chop them in pieces, as for the pot, and as flesh within the caldron.

1. Praise the Lord for the power in His name at which every knee must bow.
2. Every wicked pot cooking my affairs, be roasted, in the name of Jesus.
3. Every witchcraft pot working against me, I bring the judgement of God against you, in the name of Jesus.
4. My place of birth will not be my caldron, in Jesus' name.
5. This city where I live, will not be my caldron, in Jesus' name.
6. Every pot of darkness, seated against my life, be destroyed by fire, in the name of Jesus.
7. I command every witchcraft pot, using remote control against my health, to be broken into pieces, in the name of Jesus.
8. Every power, calling my name into any caldrons, fall down and

die, in the name of Jesus.

9. Every caldron, making noise against me and monitoring my life, disintegrate, in the name of Jesus.
10. Every power, cooking my progress in an evil pot, receive the fire of judgement, in the name of Jesus.
11. Every satanic programme, emanating from the caldron of darkness, be reversed, in the name of Jesus.
12. Any evil fire, boiling any satanic programme in my life, be quenched, in the name of Jesus.
13. The counsel of the wicked, against my life in this city, shall not stand and I command them to perish, in Jesus' name.
14. Let the counsel of God for my life prosper, in Jesus' name.
15. Every power cooking my flesh and my health in any evil caldron, receive the fire of God, in the name of Jesus.
16. Every evil bird of satanic programme, emanating from any caldron of darkness, fall down and die, in the name of Jesus.
17. Every pot cooking my affairs, the Lord rebuke you, in the name of Jesus.
18. I rebuke the spell of any witchcraft pot from my neck, in the name of Jesus.
19. I break every witchcraft pot over my life, in the name of Jesus.

20. Let every evil pot hunt their owners, in the name of Jesus.

21. Mention the names of the items listed below one by one and pray in this format: **I release my life from your caldron, in the name of the Lord Jesus Christ.**

- blood hunters
- eaters of flesh and drinkers of blood
- household witchcraft
- star hunters
- mischief planners
- blood polluters
- envious witchcraft
- destiny killers
- health destroyers
- priests operating on evil altars

22. Every evil caldron or pot, be judged from heaven, in the name of Jesus.

23. No evil caldron will cook up my life, in the name of Jesus.

24. Every council of witchcraft working against me will not prosper, in the name of Jesus.

25. Every agreement with satan over my life, I cancel you now, in the name of Jesus.

26. Every astral projection against me, I frustrate you, in the name of Jesus.

27. I disentangle myself and my family from every witchcraft cage and pot, in the name of Jesus.

28. Every enemy that will not let me go easily, I bring the

judgement of death against you, in the name of Jesus.

29. This year, my blessings will not sink, in the name of Jesus.

30. Let the spirit of salvation fall upon my family, in the name of Jesus.

WARFARE NUMBER 12

PRAYERS TO OVERCOME WITCHCRAFT

Psalm 59:1-17: Deliver me from mine enemies, O my God: defend me from them that rise up against me. Deliver me from the workers of iniquity, and save me from bloody men. For, lo, they lie in wait for my soul: the mighty are gathered against me; not for my transgression, nor for my sin, O Lord. They run and prepare themselves without my fault: awake to help me, and behold. Thou therefore, O Lord God of hosts, the God of Israel, awake to visit all the heathen: be not merciful to any wicked transgressors. Selah. They return at evening: they make a noise like a dog, and go round about the city. Behold, they belch out with their mouth: swords are in their lips: for who, say they, doth hear? But thou, Oh Lord, shalt laugh at them; thou shalt have all the heathen in derision. Because of his strength will I wait upon thee: for God is my defence. The God of my mercy shall prevent me: God shall let me see my desire upon mine enemies. Slay them not, lest my people forget: scatter them by thy power; and bring them down, O Lord our shield. For the sin of their mouth and the words of their lips let them even be taken in their pride: and for cursing and lying which they speak. Consume them in wrath, consume them, that they may not be: and let them know that God ruleth in Jacob unto the ends of the earth. Selah. And at evening let them return; and let them make a noise like a dog, and go round about the city. Let them wander up and down for meat, and grudge if they be not satisfied. But I will sing of thy power; yea,

I will sing aloud of thy mercy in the morning: for thou hast been my defence and refuge in the day of my trouble. Unto thee, O my strength, will I sing: for God is my defence, and the God of my mercy.

Aggressive praise worship

1. Let every problem in my life, that originated from witchcraft, receive divine instant solution in the name of Jesus.
2. I command the damage, done to my life, by witchcraft to be repaired in the name of Jesus.
3. Let every blessing, confiscated by witchcraft spirits, be released in Jesus' name.
4. Every witchcraft power assigned against my life and marriage, receive . . . (pick from the under listed), in the name of Jesus.
   - the thunder and lightning of God
   - hail and fire mingled with the Blood of the Lamb
   - unbearable heat
   - concentrated acid
   - destroying flood
   - destruction
   - raging fire
   - continuous plagues
   - failures
   - confusion
5. I loose myself from any power of witchcraft in the name of Jesus.

6. Every camp of witchcraft gathered against my prosperity, fall down and die, in Jesus' name.
7. Every witchcraft pot working against me, I bring the judgment of God against you, in the name of Jesus.
8. I command every witchcraft pot, using remote control against my health to be broken into pieces, in the name of Jesus.
9. Witchcraft opposition, receive the rain of affliction, in the name of Jesus.
10. Let the spirit of witchcraft attack and familiar spirits fashioned against me backfire, in Jesus' name.
11. I retrieve my integrity out of the hands of household witchcraft, in the name of Jesus.
12. I break the power of the occult, witchcraft and familiar spirits over my life, in Jesus' name.
13. In the name of Jesus, I break and loose myself from all evil curses, chains, spells, jinx, bewitchments, witchcraft or sorcery which may have been put upon me.
14. Let the thunder of God, locate and dismantle the throne of witchcraft in my household, in the name of Jesus.
15. Let every seat of witchcraft, in my household be roasted with the fire of God, in Jesus' name.
16. Let the altar of witchcraft in my household be roasted, in the

name of Jesus.

17. Let the thunder of God, scatter beyond redemption, the foundation of witchcraft in my household, in the name of Jesus.

18. Every stronghold of refuge of my household witches, be destroyed, in the name of Jesus.

19. Every hiding and secret places of witchcraft in my family, be exposed by fire, in the name of Jesus.

20. Let every local and international witchcraft network of my household witches be shattered into pieces, in the name of Jesus.

21. Let the communication system of my household witches be frustrated, in the name of Jesus.

22. Let the terrible fire of God, consume the transportation of my household witchcraft, in the name of Jesus.

23. Every agent, ministering at the altar of witchcraft, in my household, fall down and die, in the name of Jesus.

24. Let the thunder and the fire of God, locate the storehouses and strongrooms of my household witchcraft harbouring my blessings, and pull them down, in the name of Jesus.

25. Let any witchcraft curse working against me be revoked by the blood of Jesus.

26. Every decision, vow and covenant of household witchcraft affecting me, be nullified by the blood of Jesus.
27. I destroy with the fire of God, every weapon of witchcraft used against me, in Jesus' name.
28. Any material taken from my body, now placed on a witchcraft altar, be roasted by the fire of God, in the name of Jesus.
29. I reverse every witchcraft burial fashioned against me, in the name of Jesus.
30. Every trap, set for me by witches begin to catch your owners, in the name of Jesus.
31. Every witchcraft padlock, fashioned against any area of my life, be roasted, in Jesus' name.
32. Let the wisdom of my household witches be converted to foolishness, in the name of Jesus.
33. Let the wickedness of my household enemies overtake them, in the name of Jesus.
34. I deliver my soul from every witchcraft bewitchment, in the name of Jesus.
35. Any witchcraft bird flying for my sake, fall down, die and be roasted to ashes, in the name of Jesus.
36. Any of my blessings traded with by household witches be returned to me, in Jesus' name.

37. Any of my blessings and testimonies swallowed by witches, be converted to hot coals of fire of God and be vomited, in the name of Jesus.

38. I break myself loose from every bondage of witchcraft covenants, in the name of Jesus.

39. Any witchcraft coven where any of my blessings are hidden, be roasted by the fire of God, in the name of Jesus.

40. (Lay your right hand on your head) Every witchcraft spirit plantation, pollution, deposit and material in my body, melt by the fire of God and be flushed out by the blood of Jesus.

41. Every evil ever done to me through witchcraft attack, be reversed, in the name of Jesus.

42. Every witchcraft hand, planting evil seeds in my life through attacks in the dream, wither and burn to ashes, in the name of Jesus.

43. Every witchcraft obstacle and hindrance put on the road to my desired miracle and success, be removed by the east wind of God, in the name of Jesus.

44. Every witchcraft chant, spell and projection made against me, I bind you and turn you against your owner, in the name of Jesus.

45. I frustrate every plot, device, scheme and project of

witchcraft designed to affect any area of my life, in the name of Jesus.

46. Any witch projecting himself into the body of any animal in order to do me harm or evil, be trapped in the body of such an animal forever, in the name of Jesus.

47. Any drop of my blood sucked by any witch, be vomited now, in the name of Jesus.

48. Any part of me shared out amongst household / village witches, I recover you, in the name of Jesus.

49. Any organ of my body that has been exchanged for another through witchcraft operations, be replaced now, in the name of Jesus.

50. I recover any of my virtues / blessings shared out amongst village / household witches, in the name of Jesus.

51. I reverse the evil effect of any witchcraft invocation or summoning of my spirit, in the name of Jesus.

52. I loose my hands and feet from any witchcraft bewitchment and bondage, in Jesus' name.

53. Let the blood of Jesus wash away from my life every witchcraft identification mark on me or on any of my property, in Jesus' name.

54. I forbid any re-union or re-gathering of household and village

witches against my life, in the name of Jesus.

55.Let the entire body system of my household witches begin to run contrary until they have confessed all their wickedness, in Jesus' name.

56.Let the mercy of God be withdrawn from them, in the name of Jesus.

57.Let them begin to grope in the daytime as in the thickness of a dark night, in the name of Jesus.

58.Let everything that has ever worked for them begin to work against them, in Jesus' name.

59.Let them not have a cloth to cover their shame, in the name of Jesus.

60.Let as many of them as are stubbornly unrepentant be smitten by the sun in the day and by the moon in the night, in Jesus' name.

61. Let each step they take lead them to greater destruction, in the name of Jesus.

62.But as for me, let me dwell in the hollow of God's hand, in the name of Jesus.

63.Let the goodness and mercy of God now overwhelm me, in the name of Jesus.

64.Any witchcraft practise under any water against my life,

receive immediate judgment of fire, in the name of Jesus.

65. Every witchcraft power that has introduced spirit husband/wife or child into my dreams, be roasted by fire, in the name of Jesus.

66. Every agent of witchcraft power posing as my husband, wife or child in my dreams, be roasted by fire, in the name of Jesus.

67. Every agent of witchcraft power physically attached to my marriage to frustrate it, fall down and perish now, in the name of Jesus.

68. Every agent of witchcraft power assigned to attack my finances through the dream, fall down and perish, in the name of Jesus.

69. Let the thunderbolts of God locate and destroy every witchcraft power covens where deliberations and decisions are fashioned against me, in the name of Jesus.

70. Any water spirit from my village, in my place of birth, practising witchcraft against me and family, be amputated by the Word of God, in the name of Jesus.

71. Any power of witchcraft holding any of my blessings in bondage, receive the fire of God and release them, in the name of Jesus.

72.I loose my mind and soul from the bondage of marine witches, in the name of Jesus.

73.Any witchcraft power chain, binding my hands and feet from prospering, be broken and shattered into pieces, in the name of Jesus.

74.Every arrow shot into my life from under any water through witchcraft, come out of me and go back to your sender, in the name of Jesus.

75.Any evil material transferred into my body through contact with any witchcraft agent, be roasted by fire, in the name of Jesus.

76.Any evil done against me so far, through witchcraft power oppression and manipulation, be reversed by the blood of Jesus.

77.I bind every witchcraft control and mind-blinding spirit, in the name of Jesus.

78.I cast out every witchcraft arrow affecting my senses (sight, smell, taste, hearing), in the name of Jesus.

79.I command every witchcraft arrow to depart from my ___, in the name of Jesus.

- spinal cord
- spleen
- navel
- heart
- throat

- eyes - top of the head

80. Let the blood of Jesus purge me of every witchcraft contaminating material, in the name of Jesus.
81. I destroy the hand of any witch-doctor working against me, in the name of Jesus.
82. Every witchcraft spirit attempting to build a wall against my destiny, fall down and die, in the name of Jesus.
83. I send the rain of affliction, upon every witchcraft power working against me, in the name of Jesus.
84. Oh sun, moon, stars, earth, water and the elements, vomit every enchantment that is against me, in the name of Jesus
85. Every power using the heavenlies against me, fall down and be disgraced, in Jesus' name.
86. Let the stars of heaven begin to fight for me, in the name of Jesus.
87. Oh God, arise and scatter every conspiracy in the heavenlies that is against me, in Jesus' name.
88. I break with the blood of Jesus all evil soul-ties affecting my life, in the name of Jesus.
89. Spirit of the living God, come upon my life and place a shield of protection around me, in the name of Jesus.
90. Every chain of inherited witchcraft in my family, break, in the

name of Jesus.

91. Every ladder used by witchcraft against me, be roasted, in the name of Jesus.

92. Any door that I have opened to witchcraft in any area of my life, be closed for ever by the blood of Jesus.

93. I revoke every witchcraft verdict on my marital life, in the name of Jesus.

94. I send confusion into the camp of household witchcraft, in the name of Jesus.

95. Stubborn witchcraft, release me, in the name of Jesus.

96. Every witchcraft power working against my destiny, fall down and die, in Jesus' name.

97. Every incantation, ritual and witchcraft power against my destiny, fall down and die, in the name of Jesus.

98. I break the power of the occult, witchcraft and familiar spirits over my life, in Jesus' name.

99. Witchcraft opposition, receive the rain of affliction, in the name of Jesus.

100. I cancel every witchcraft verdict against my life, in the name of Jesus.

101. I command every arrow of witchcraft in my life, come out with all your roots in the name of Jesus! (Lay your hands on

your stomach and pray aggressively.)

102. I command every witchcraft pot using remote control against my health to be broken into pieces, in the name of Jesus.

103. I rebuke the spell of any witchcraft pot from my neck, in the name of Jesus.

104. I break every witchcraft pot over my life, in the name of Jesus.

105. Every council of witchcraft working against me will not prosper, in the name of Jesus.

106. I release myself and my family from every witchcraft cage and pot, in the name of Jesus.

107. I retrieve my integrity out of the hands of household witchcraft, in the name of Jesus.

108. Every witchcraft hand, planting evil seeds in my life through attack in the dream, wither and burn to ashes, in the name of Jesus.

109. Let all friendly witchcraft powers be exposed and disgraced, in the name of Jesus.

110. Oh Lord, plant Your warring angels around me to dismantle and destroy evil stronghold of internal witchcraft.

111. I exercise my authority over stubborn witchcraft and I

pull down their structures, in Jesus' name.

112. Every placenta witchcraft targeted against my destiny, what are you waiting for? die, in the name of Jesus.

113. Placenta witchcraft manipulating my destiny, die, in the name of Jesus.

114. Every blessing that I have lost through placenta witchcraft, I possess you, in Jesus' name.

115. Every witchcraft coven and marine bank, release my placenta, in Jesus' name

116. Every cage of family witchcraft, release my divine partner, in Jesus' name.

117. Oh Lord, let my dreams and visions reject every witchcraft projection, in the name of Jesus.

118. Thank God for answers to prayers.

WARFARE NUMBER 13

POWER AGAINST MARINE WITCHCRAFT

Ezek 29:1-3: "In the tenth year, in the tenth month, in the twelfth day of the month, the word of the LORD came unto me, saying, Son of man, set thy face against Pharaoh king of Egypt, and prophesy against him, and against all Egypt: Speak, and say, Thus saith the Lord GOD; Behold, I am against thee, Pharaoh king of Egypt, the great dragon that lieth in the midst of his rivers, which hath said, My river is mine own, and I have made it for myself."

I go into this prayer, I hold in my hand the victory Jesus Christ purchased on the cross at Calvary, when He made an open show of principality and powers. I take my position in Christ as one given power to become a son of God, even joint heir with Christ of the kingdom of God, to execute judgment against every form of disobedience exhibited against the knowledge of God.

Greater is He that is in me than any power on earth and in the seas. I am born of God, and I have overcome the world with my faith.

In faith, I hand over my battle to God. In faith, I come against evil strongholds of any marine kingdom. In faith, I pollute your water with the blood of Jesus Christ. In faith, I overturn every queen enthroned against me. In faith, I trample upon her serpents and scorpions. In faith, I spoil her palace and set her captives free and bind her herself.

There shall be no reinforcement or evil reunion of this power against me. I seal my confessions with the blood of Jesus and I cover myself with the blood of Jesus. Amen.

PRAISE WORSHIP

1. Any witchcraft practised under any water against my life, receive immediate judgment of fire, in the name of Jesus.
2. Let every evil altar under any water upon which certain evils are done against me, be roasted, in the name of Jesus.
3. Every priest, ministering at any evil altar against me inside any water, fall down and die, in the name of Jesus.
4. Any power under any river or sea remotely-controlling my life, be destroyed by fire, and I shake myself loose from your hold, in the name of Jesus.
5. Let any evil monitoring mirror ever used against me under any water, crush to irredeemable pieces, in the name of Jesus.
6. Every marine witchcraft that has introduced spirit husband/wife or child in my dreams be roasted by fire, in the name of Jesus.
7. Every agent of marine witchcraft posing as my husband, wife or child in my dreams, be roasted by fire, in the name of Jesus.
8. Every agent of marine witchcraft physically attached to my

marriage to frustrate it, fall down and perish now, in Jesus' name.

9. Every agent of marine witchcraft assigned to attack my finances through the dream, fall down and perish, in the name of Jesus.

10. I pull down every stronghold of bewitchment, enchantment, jinx or divination fashioned against me by marine witches, in Jesus' name.

11. Let the thunderbolts of God, locate and destroy every marine witchcraft covens where deliberations and decisions have ever been fashioned against me, in the name of Jesus.

12. Any water spirit from my village or my place of birth, practising witchcraft against me and my family, be amputated by the word of God, in the name of Jesus.

13. Let every spiritual weapon of wickedness fashioned against me under any river or sea, be roasted by the fire of God, in the name of Jesus.

14. Any power of marine witchcraft holding any of my blessings in bondage, receive the fire of God and release them, in Jesus' name.

15. I loose my mind and soul from the bondage of marine witches, in the name of Jesus.

16. Any marine witchcraft chain binding my hands and feet from prospering, be broken and shattered into pieces, in Jesus' name.
17. Every arrow shot into my life from under any water by witchcraft powers, come out of me and go back to your sender, in the name of Jesus.
18. Any evil material transferred into my body through contact with any marine witchcraft agent, be roasted by fire, in the name of Jesus.
19. Every sexual pollution of marine spirit husband/wife in my body, be flushed out by the blood of Jesus.
20. Any evil name given to me under any water, I reject and cancel it with the blood of Jesus.
21. Every image constructed under any water to manipulate me, be roasted by fire, in the name of Jesus.
22. Any evil ever done against me through marine witchcraft oppression and manipulation, be reversed by the blood of Jesus.

WARFARE NUMBER 14

PRAYERS TO ARREST ANTI-PROGRESS FORCES

Confession: Isaiah 49:25: But thus saith the Lord, Even the captives of the mighty shall be taken away, and the prey of the terrible shall be delivered: for I will contend with him that contendeth with thee, and I will save thy children.

Praise Worship

1. Lord, I thank You for Your power that is able to deliver from every form of bondage and from every form of demonic oppression, in the name of Jesus.
2. I confess every sin of my ancestors, and I ask for forgiveness for all my sins by the blood of Jesus.
3. I plead the blood of Jesus over my life and this environment, in the name of Jesus.
4. I renounce every evil dedication placed upon my life, by the blood of Jesus.
5. I break every evil edict and ordinance assigned against my progress, in the name of Jesus.
6. I renounce and loose myself from every negative dedication placed upon my life, in the name of Jesus.
7. I command all demons associated with any evil dedication operating in my life to leave now, in the name of Jesus.
8. I take authority over and revoke, all the associated curses, in the name of Jesus.

9. I cancel all the evil consequences of broken demonic promises or dedications in my life, in the name of Jesus.
10. I take authority over all the curses emanating from broken dedications, initiations, covenants, engagements, and vows, in the name of Jesus.
11. Every ancestral curse operating in my life, be removed by the blood of Jesus.
12. I command any demon afflicting me or causing stagnation in my life to leave now, in the name of Jesus.
13. Let the blood of Jesus heal every spiritual and physical wound in my life, in the name of Jesus.
14. Every stronghold of thought, image and pictures of failure in my heart, be pulled down by fire, in the name of Jesus.
15. I reject every spirit of doubt, fear and discouragement, in the name of Jesus.
16. All ungodly delay to the manifestation of my miracles, scatter, in the name of Jesus.
17. Let the angels of the Living God roll away all stones of hindrance to the manifestations of my breakthroughs, in the name of Jesus.
18. Oh Lord, avenge me of my adversaries speedily, in the name of Jesus.

19. Every dark power assigned against my progress in life, be arrested, in the name of Jesus.

20. Let situations and circumstances within me, around me and over me, be re-routed to favour my desired miracles today, in the name of Jesus.

21. O God that quickened Sarah and called those things that are not, as if they were, arise and answer me by fire, in the name of Jesus.

22. Let the blood of Jesus flow into my situation and revoke all unholy alliances and ordinances working against my life, in the name of Jesus.

23. Every evil design against my life, be cancelled by the blood of Jesus.

24. I use the blood of Jesus to wipe out all evil labels of the enemy fashioned against my life, in the name of Jesus.

25. I drink the blood of Jesus and I vomit all satanic deposits in my body, in the name of Jesus.

26. I break myself loose from the bondage of life stagnation, in the name of Jesus.

27. Everything that is making the promises of God to fail in my life, I renounce you today, get out of my life, in the name of Jesus.

28.I use the blood of Jesus to uproot every unprofitable growth in my life, in the name of Jesus.

29.I use the blood of Jesus to cancel every evil plantation, parental contamination and evil spiritual contamination in my life, in the name of Jesus.

30.Blood of Jesus, cleanse all hidden sicknesses, evil stamps and labels of the enemies from my life, in the name of Jesus.

31. I reverse, every evil arrangement setup for my life, in the name of Jesus.

32.Every evil manipulation and evil manipulators, assigned against my life, scatter, in the name of Jesus.

33.I break myself free from all powers of the occult, witchcraft and familiar spirits, in the name of Jesus.

34.I release myself from every satanic dream plantation, in the name of Jesus.

35.Every satanic deposit, in my reproductive organs, be flushed out by the blood of Jesus.

36.I release myself from the grip of my adversaries, in the name of Jesus.

37.I bind and cast out of my life, every spirit of demonic oppression, in the name of Jesus.

38.I bind and cast out of my life, every spirit of spiritual dryness, in the name of Jesus.

39. I bind and cast out of my life, every spirit of lukewarmness, in the name of Jesus.

40. I bind and cast out of my life, every spirit of non-achievement, in the name of Jesus.

41. I bind and cast out of my life, every spirit of limitation, in the name of Jesus.

42. I bind and cast out of my life, every spirit of frustration, in the name of Jesus.

43. I bind and cast out of my life, every spirit of failure at the edge of breakthroughs, in the name of Jesus.

44. Every curse, chain, spell, jinx, bewitchment, assigned against my progress, die, in the name of Jesus.

45. Let the creative miracle of God begin to take place in my body, in the name of Jesus.

46. All witchcraft burial assigned against my progress, catch fire, in the name of Jesus.

47. Every strongman assigned against my progress, fall down and die, in the name of Jesus.

48. Every infirmity assigned to hinder my progress, die, in the name of Jesus.

49. Every activity of spiritual wickedness in high places assigned

against my progress, scatter, in the name of Jesus.

50. Every manipulation of my increase and productivity, die, in the name of Jesus.

WARFARE NUMBER 15

DELIVERANCE PRAYERS FROM WITCHCRAFT OPERATIONS

Confession: Matthew 18:18: Verily I say unto you, Whatsoever ye shall bind on earth shall be bound in heaven: and whatsoever ye shall loose on earth shall be loosed in heaven.

Praise Worship

1. Lord, I thank You for Your power that is able to deliver from every form of bondage and from every form of demonic oppression, in the name of Jesus.
2. I come against all the demonic sleeping waves that make me to feel sleepy when I do not intend to sleep in the house and church service, giving room for the enemy to operate against me, in the name of Jesus.
3. Every evil mark or tattoo on my body, face or hands, being used for evil identification wherever I go, be wiped out by the blood of Jesus.
4. All hidden evil marks in my body, be wiped out by the blood of Jesus.
5. Every witchcraft food or drink I have taken in the dreams, I neutralize and flush it out by the blood of Jesus.
6. Every witchcraft blackboard, witchcraft computers, witchcraft red book, witchcraft book of death, containing my name, catch fire, in the name of Jesus.
7. Every witchcraft padlock, used to lock doors of my

supernatural and physical breakthroughs, in the air, land or sea, catch fire and break into pieces, in the name of Jesus.

8. I receive the master key to unlock the doors of my breakthroughs, in the name of Jesus.
9. Every witchcraft diversion of my life, favour and greatness, die, in the name of Jesus.
10. All agents of evil diversion assigned against my life and progress, fall down and die, in the name of Jesus.
11. Every witchcraft broom used to sweep away my favour, progress, breakthroughs, prosperity, finances and marriage, catch fire now, in the name of Jesus.
12. Every agent of satan, assigned to be using brooms to sweep away my blessings, fall down and die, in the name of Jesus.
13. Let the Holy Ghost fire come upon the witchcraft brooms used to sweep sicknesses, weakness, poverty, failure, troubles, bitterness, hatred, misfortune into my life, in the name of Jesus.
14. I reject every evil load of affliction, depression, family strife and suffering brought by witchcraft into my life, I send them back to the senders, in the name of Jesus.
15. Let torment come upon the witchcraft power that has swallowed my destiny, prayers, blessings, favour, promotion,

children and opportunities, to vomit them now, in the name of Jesus.

16. Let the witchcraft agents assigned against my life begin to chase themselves, in the name of Jesus.

17. Every poison of the enemy that I inhaled, be neutralized by the blood of Jesus.

18. Let all hidden wickedness in my family be exposed, in the name of Jesus.

19. All wickedness assigned against my progress, die, in the name of Jesus.

20. Any witchcraft meeting assigned against me in the air, land or sea, scatter, in the name of Jesus.

21. Every witchcraft manipulation of my life, destiny, character, career, progress, success, and favour, die, in the name of Jesus.

22. Any witchcraft power, that has stolen from me, in the dream, be arrested now, in the name of Jesus.

23. Let every evil plantation planted in my life, be uprooted by fire now, in the name of Jesus.

24. Every seed of suffering, failure, poverty, backwardness in life, death, illness, beggarly life, in my life, be uprooted, in the name of Jesus.

25. Every witchcraft incantation, invocations, enchantment, evil songs, and mischievous words spoken against me, die, in the name of Jesus.

26. Let the pit dug for me catch its diggers, in the name of Jesus.

27. Any witchcraft prison, where my spirit, soul and body are serving unjust terms, catch fire, and let me go, in the name of Jesus.

28. Any witchcraft tree in the forest assigned against my life, catch fire, in the name of Jesus.

29. Any witchcraft effigy molded for my sake, fall down and die, in the name of Jesus.

30. Every witchcraft storm bringing problems, sickness, failures, loss of wealth, death, miscarriage of blessings into my life, stop and die, in the name of Jesus.

31. I decree continuous bombardment of witchcraft detention camp until they discharge and acquit me and my entire family from their detention camp, in the name of Jesus.

32. I decree paralysis upon every spirit of re-enforcement in my life, family and ministry, in the name of Jesus.

33. Every witchcraft agent, sent to monitor my progress in the house or office, receive blindness, in the name of Jesus.

34. Every witchcraft devourer, assigned against my life, devour

yourselves, in the name of Jesus.

35. Begin to thank God for answers to your prayers.

WARFARE NUMBER 16

PRAYERS TO SUBDUE WITCHCRAFT OPERATIONS

Confession: Col. 1:20: And, having made peace through the blood of his cross, by him to reconcile all things unto himself; by him, I say, whether they be things in earth, or things in heaven.

Praise Worship

1. Lord, I thank You for Your power that is able to deliver from every form of bondage and from every form of demonic oppression, in the name of Jesus.
2. Father, I worship You for opening my eyes to the subject of subduing witchcraft gates in the land.
3. Father, I repent for my carelessness and negligence of witchcraft activities in my life, family, the church, and in the nations, in the name of Jesus.
4. Oh Lord, destroy lies and falsehood in our land, in the name of Jesus.
5. Oh Lord, arise and judge the seat of immorality in my neighborhood, in the name of Jesus.
6. Every form of hypnotism working in my city, I paralyse you, in the name of Jesus.
7. Oh Lord, expose the architects of bribery and corruption in our cities and nations, in the name of Jesus.
8. Any man or woman sitting in an effort to make me a physical and spiritual eunuch, fall now, in the name of Jesus.

9. Every spirit of carelessness and excessive pleasure in my life, die, in the name of Jesus.
10. Oh Lord, let every manipulation of the sun, the moon and the stars against me and my family die, in the name of Jesus.
11. Oh Lord, let every enchantment and sorcery against me not see the light of the day, in the name of Jesus.
12. Father, arise and cut off the spirit of divination in my neighborhood, in the name of Jesus.
13. I receive strength to paralyse every form of witchcraft in my neighborhood, in the name of Jesus.
14. Father, I pray that You visit the thrones in this nation by Yourself, in the name of Jesus.
15. Lord, let the bewitchment over my city be broken and let the instruments of such bewitchment lose their grip, in the name of Jesus.
16. Lord, deliver Your appointed leaders and me from the spirit of pride, in the name of Jesus.
17. Oh Lord, open the eyes of our leaders to the buying and selling of nations by the mistress of witchcraft, in the name of Jesus.
18. Lord, give the church spiritual understanding in the marketplace, in the name of Jesus.

19. Oh Lord, I pray that by the help of the Holy Spirit, You expose those men given to ritual killings in our cities, in the name of Jesus.

20. Lord, use me to judge witchcraft operations in my workplace, in the name of Jesus.

21. I destroy every covering of darkness over all my investments and other life endeavors, in the name of Jesus.

22. Every object or animal around me that facilitates witchcraft attack, I command you to receive God's fire of judgement, in the name of Jesus.

23. Father, let the eyes of the church, be opened, to the need to take responsibility for waging the war against the mistress of witchcraft in our media houses, in the name of Jesus.

24. Every spiritual cobweb put on my office, my home, my ministry and my life, catch fire, in the name of Jesus.

25. Oh Lord, give the church the grace to watch both day and night, in the name of Jesus.

26. Father, I silence the voice of necromancers in my family and city, in the name of Jesus.

27. Lord, arise and deliver our leaders from spiritual bewitchment, in the name of Jesus.

28. I dethrone the seat of witchcraft operations in my

neighborhood and city, in the name of Jesus.

29. Lord, for the blood shed in my neighborhood and city, have mercy, Father; let the lives of men be precious to us as city dwellers, in the name of Jesus.

30. Oh Lord, give me the burden to pray against the mistress of witchcraft, in the name of Jesus.

31. Father, I receive the boldness to tame witchcraft activities, in the name of Jesus.

32. Oh Lord, wake up the church, in the place of prayer, to watch over our land, in the name of Jesus.

33. Oh Lord, release a spiritual broom, to sweep witchcraft activities out of our cities, in the name of Jesus.

34. Lord, I receive the discerning spirit today to unravel the deceptions of witchcraft spirit, in the name of Jesus.

35. Every manipulation of witchcraft spirit against my life, break, in the name of Jesus.

36. Oh Lord, teach my hands to war in my city, in the name of Jesus.

37. Oh Lord, give me the appetite for prayers, in the name of Jesus.

38. Begin to thank God.

OTHER PUBLICATIONS BY THE GENERAL OVERSEER

1. 20 Marching Orders To Fulfill Your Destiny
2. 30 Things The Anointing Can Do For You
3. A-Z of Complete Deliverance
4. Abraham's Children in Bondage
5. Be Prepared
6. Bewitchment must die
7. Biblical Principles of Dream Interpretation
8. Born Great, But Tied Down
9. Breaking Bad Habits
10. Breakthrough Prayers For Business Professionals
11. Brokenness
12. Bringing Down The Power of God
13. Can God?
14. Can God Trust You?
15. Command The Morning
16. Consecration Commitment & Loyalty
17. Contending For The Kingdom
18. Connecting to The God of Breakthroughs
19. Criminals In The House Of God
20. Dancers At The Gate of Death
21. Dealing With Hidden Curses
22. Dealing With Local Satanic Technology
23. Dealing With Satanic Exchange
24. Dealing With The Evil Powers Of Your Father's House

25. Dealing With Tropical Demons
26. Dealing With Unprofitable Roots
27. Dealing With Witchcraft Barbers
28. Deliverance By Fire
29. Deliverance From Spirit Husband And Spirit Wife
30. Deliverance From The Limiting Powers
31. Deliverance of The Brain
32. Deliverance Of The Conscience
33. Deliverance Of The Head
34. Deliverance of The Tongue
35. Deliverance: God's Medicine Bottle
36. Destiny Clinic
37. Destroying Satanic Masks
38. Disgracing Soul Hunters
39. Divine Military Training
40. Divine Yellow Card
41. Dominion Prosperity
42. Drawers Of Power From The Heavenlies
43. Evil Appetite
44. Evil Umbrella
45. Facing Both Ways
46. Failure In The School Of Prayer
47. Fire For Life's Journey
48. For We Wrestle ...
49. Freedom Indeed

50. God's Key To A Happy Life
51. Holiness Unto The Lord
52. Holy Cry
53. Holy Fever
54. Hour Of Decision
55. How To Obtain Personal Deliverance
56. How To Pray When Surrounded By The Enemies
57. Idols Of The Heart
58. Is This What They Died For?
59. Killing The Serpent of Frustration
60. Let God Answer By Fire
61. Lord, Behold Their Threatening
62. Limiting God
63. Madness Of The Heart
64. Making Your Way Through The Traffic Jam of Life
65. Meat For Champions
66. Medicine For Winners
67. My Burden For The Church
68. Open Heavens Through Holy Disturbance
69. Overpowering Witchcraft
70. Paralysing The Riders And The Horse
71. Personal Spiritual Check-Up
72. Possessing The Tongue of Fire
73. Power Against Coffin Spirits
74. Power Against Destiny Quenchers

100. Setting The Covens Ablaze
101. Seventy Sermons To Preach To Your Destiny
102. Silencing The Birds Of Darkness
103. Slaves Who Love Their Chains
104. Smite The Enemy And He Will Flee
105. Speaking Destruction Unto The Dark Rivers
106. Spiritual Education
107. Spiritual Growth And Maturity
108. Spiritual Warfare And The Home
109. Strategic Praying
110. Strategy Of Warfare Praying
111. Stop Them Before They Stop You
112. Students In The School Of Fear
113. Symptoms Of Witchcraft Attack
114. The Baptism of Fire
115. The Battle Against The Spirit Of Impossibility
116. The Dinning Table Of Darkness
117. The Enemy Has Done This
118. The Evil Cry Of Your Family Idol
119. The Fire Of Revival
120. The Great Deliverance
121. The Internal Stumbling Block
122. The Lord Is A Man Of War
123. The Mystery Of Mobile Curses
124. The Mystery Of The Mobile Temple

125. The Prayer Eagle
126. The Power of Aggressive Prayer Warriors
127. The Power of Priority
128. The Pursuit Of Success
129. The Seasons Of Life
130. The Secrets Of Greatness
131. The Serpentine Enemies
132. The Skeleton In Your Grandfather's Cupboard
133. The Slow Learners
134. The Snake In The Power House
135. The Spirit Of The Crab
136. The star hunters
137. The Star In Your Sky
138. The Terrible Agenda
139. The Tongue Trap
140. The Unconquerable Power
141. The Unlimited God
142. The Vagabond Spirit
143. The Way Of Divine Encounter
144. The Wealth Transfer Agenda
145. Tied Down In The Spirits
146. Too Hot To Handle
147. Turnaround Breakthrough
148. Unprofitable Foundations
149. Victory Over Satanic Dreams

150. Victory Over Your Greatest Enemies
151. Violent Prayers Against Stubborn Situations
152. War At The Edge Of Breakthroughs
153. Wasting The Wasters
154. Wasted At The Market Square of Life
155. Wealth Must Change Hands
156. What You Must Know About The House Fellowship
157. When God Is Silent
158. When the Battle is from Home
159. When The Deliverer Need Deliverance
160. When Things Get Hard
161. When You Are Knocked Down
162. Where Is Your Faith
163. While Men Slept
164. Woman! Thou Art Loosed.
165. Your Battle And Your Strategy
166. Your Foundation And Destiny
167. Your Mouth And Your Deliverance

YORUBA PUBLICATIONS

1. ADURA AGBAYORI
2. ADURA TI NSI OKE NIDI
3. OJO ADURA

FRENCH PUBLICATIONS

26. DEMANTELER LA SORCELLERIES
27. LA DELIVERANCE: LE FLACON DE MEDICAMENT DIEU
28. LA DELIVERANCE DE LA TETE
29. COMMANDER LE MATIN
30. NE GRAND MAIS LIE
31. POUVOIR CONTRE LES DEMOND TROPICAUX
32. LE PROGRAMME DE TRANFERT DE RICHESSE
33. LES ETUDIANTS A I'ECOLE DE LA PEUR
34. L'ETOILE DANS VOTRE CIEL
35. LES SAISONS DE LA VIE
36. FEMME TU ES LIBEREE

ANNUAL 70 DAYS PRAYER AND FASTING PUBLICATIONS

1. Prayers That Bring Miracles
2. Let God Answer By Fire
3. Prayers to Mount With Wings As Eagles
4. Prayers That Bring Explosive Increase
5. Prayers For Open Heavens
6. Prayers To Make You Fulfill Your Divine Destiny
7. Prayers That Make God To Answer And Fight By Fire
8. Prayers That Bring Unchallengeable Victory And Breakthrough Rainfall Bombardments
9. Prayers That Bring Dominion Prosperity And Uncommon Success
10. Prayers That Bring Power And Overflowing Progress
11. Prayers That Bring Laughter And Enlargement Breakthroughs
12. Prayers That Bring Uncommon Favour And Breakthroughs
13. Prayers That Bring Unprecedented Greatness & Unmatchable Increase
14. Prayers That Bring Awesome Testimonies And Turn Around Breakthroughs
15. Prayers That Bring Glorious Restoration

about the book

SETTING THE COVENS ABLAZE

More than anytime in our generation, the powers of witchcraft are at work in our lives, families, societies, etc. Their operations affect our business, finances, economy, children and all spheres of life.

This is a classic, penned by an authority on this subject, Dr. D. K. Olukoya. This book deals extensively with witchcraft; it's signs, symptoms, manifestation, and teaches the believer how to exercise their authority over witchcraft powers.

Woe Unto Witchcraft !

about the author

Dr. D. K. Olukoya is the General Overseer of the Mountain of Fire and Miracles Ministries and The Battle Cry Christian Ministries.

The Mountain of Fire and Miracles Ministries' Headquarters is the largest single Christian congregation in Africa with attendance of over 120,000 in single meetings.

MFM is a full gospel ministry devoted to the revival of Apostolic signs, Holy Ghost Fireworks, miracles and the unlimited demonstration of the power of God to deliver to the uttermost. Absolute holiness within and without as spiritual insecticide and pre-requisite for heaven is openly taught. MFM is a do-it-yourself Gospel Ministry, where your hands are trained to wage war and your fingers to do battle.

Dr. Olukoya holds a first class honours degree in Micro-biology from the University of Lagos and a PhD in Molecular Genetics from the University of Reading, United Kingdom. As a researcher, he has over seventy scientific publications to his credit.

Anointed by God, Dr. Olukoya is a prophet, evangelist, teacher and preacher of the Word. His life and that of his wife, Shade and their son Elijah Toluwani are living proofs that all power belongs to God.

ISBN: 978-978-8424-30-7

Printed in Great Britain
by Amazon

60812363R00102